WALT KELLY'S

Pluperfect

POGO

Edited by Mrs. Walt Kelly
and Bill Crouch, Jr.

F
A Fireside Book
Published by Simon & Schuster, Inc.
New York

In memory of Cathrine Barr,
artist, author and friend.

Copyright © 1987 by the Walt Kelly Estate
A FIRESIDE BOOK
Published by Simon & Schuster, Inc.
Simon & Schuster Building, Rockefeller Center
1230 Avenue of the Americas, New York, NY 10020
FIRESIDE and colophon are registered trademarks of Simon & Schuster, Inc.

Designed by Helen Barrow
Manufactured in the United States of America
10 9 8 7 6 5 4 3 2
Library of Congress Cataloging in Publication Data
ISBN 0-671-64220-0

CONTENTS

INTRODUCTION

A few years back, an acquaintance gave me a rather dog-earred copy of *Everlovin' Pogo*, a compilation of Walt Kelly's work from the 1950s. She figured (quite accurately) that I, more than any other person she knew, would have the proper respect and appreciation for this pearl and thus it was bequethed to me. Flipping through the pages, I recalled how, as a child, I admired the art work, long before I could read. Kelly's inimitable style, the patient brush strokes, attention to detail, the amazing texture in his work, were obvious to me even in my uneducated youth. Now, a few years older and wiser, I still sense the same wonder when looking at his work, only now with a keener comprehension of the entire process.

Kelly's talent was double-edged; combined with his uncanny draftmanship came an equally sharp sense of humor. Kelly's warm and funny characters, the twisted logic and the slightly skewed look at the human condition made POGO timeless. Walt concocted characters more human than animal. He gave them opinions, personalities, quirks, and characteristics like no other cartoonist. Pogo Possum, Albert the Alligator, Porkypine, and Howland Owl were no longer swampland creatures; they were, by the grace of Kelly's brush stroke, our friends, neighbors, coworkers, and family. In this way, Walt Kelly paved the way for the likes of me and GARFIELD.

I have always avoided social comment in my work, primarily because the task of assembling the information and making sense of it seemed too awesome to tackle. For years I thought OPEC was a denture adhesive. Walt certainly didn't have any trouble grasping the world situation by the tail and giving it a firm whip. Thank goodness for his wisdom which made understandable the affairs of the world, and thank goodness for his wit which made the problems seem manageable.

I never met Walt Kelly. From what has been written and said, I know I would have loved the man. He has been called a genius by those who knew him, and though I feel this word is grossly overused, Walt Kelly qualifies for this distinction.

Thank you Walt, for your genius, and thank you, Selby Kelly and Bill Crouch, Jr., for keeping POGO alive.

JIM DAVIS, 1987

KA-PLATZ

The Delight in the Unexpected

THERE may be madness in the method, but there is reason behind the silent noise-language seen in comic strips. An old friend, the late Representative Maury Maverick of Texas, once told me that he thought comic strips were the best means to convey the sounds he heard coming out of government. He himself, a man of well-tuned ear, gave a name to the noise. He called it gobbledygook.

Striking out at pompous epic poetry one time the Reverend Charles Dodgson coined words with comic abandon and made as much sense as is probably possible with the crutch of language in "Jabberwocky."

Children are wonderful people to deal with in using language because it is not completely necessary to communicate with them. It is just as good, if entertainment is the object, to conjure. What wriggling eels of thought are roused in the minds of most of us young when the line " 'Twas brillig, and the slithy toves Did gyre and gimble in the wabe" comes splendidly into view. Lewis Carroll felt it necessary to explain this for some reason, though he was a man of some impatience. Humpty Dumpty is made to say that "brillig" means four o'clock in the afternoon — the time when people begin broiling things for dinner.

This is a theory that can be put down only to Dumpty's brash know-it-all manner. "Brillig" doesn't mean that at all to me. It means about four o'clock, all right, but it has to do with the

Pogo drawings copyright © 1962, 1963 by Walt Kelly.

"When I use a word, it means just what I choose it to mean —neither more nor less."
~Humpty Dumpty ~ Lewis Carroll

weather. However, what was probably important to Dodgson at the time was the fact that in getting Humpty Dumpty and Alice to analyze "Jabberwocky," he was able to extract several pages of delightful material from the original egghead.

The noises in comic strips — "plink," "pow," "sock," et cetera — are somewhat in this pattern. If you have a noise, you might as well have a funny noise; not that you'll have to hold your sides when you behold "plink," but I think it's about $3\frac{1}{4}$ times funnier than "crash." Who laughs at the word "bang"? It used to be very important, but "bang" doesn't have much bang anymore. The better strips are using other words. Some of them in foreign languages, for impact. Style is very important. It would not do for Steve Canyon to fall with a Li'l Abner noise. Canyon is a dignified man and a sort of status symbol in the comic strip game. Likewise, Dick Tracy could never get hit on the head with a "whacko" noise. It should be noted that noises do not usually have more than one syllable. Put a noise into several syllables, and it begins to get lively. A bucket falling down the cellar stairs is a case in point. Especially if it comes to an unexpected end, such as hitting the dog.

Thus, when noises are transposed into speech, talk gathers interest for the child if it takes on some of the color of that bucket. Incidently, "bucket" is a funnier word than "pail." If you use your ear this way and put one word after another, pretty soon, as Jim Thurber remarked on a different occasion, pretty soon you'll have a comic strip.

Inserting bounces into already formed speech, you get something like "horribobble." There is no deep meaning behind the device; it is just the same thing as wearing a lampshade at the party if your jokes are not going over. The *Pogo* speech pattern is full of noises signifying nothing more than the grunts of a determined grandfather eating corn.

We should remember that language is a tool and keep in mind Dumpty's injunction never to let the word be the master. Language not only is a tool; it is a recent and imperfect tool. In my business it should do what the child mind of any age desires it to do.

Whereas it is important to conjure up images, it must be admitted that it is also important to communicate. It is not important to communicate exact shades of meaning, but it is necessary to get across a sense of fun. Once the child understands that this is not at all a serious message, he begins to understand what's going on even if it is only his version of the proceedings. So he starts to enjoy himself, and that is the only objective.

Serious language can be carried on to such lengths that we have become a little like the Egyptians, who finally got so enmeshed in officialese that special people had to be trained to read the formal handwriting. We're in just about that shape with our legal briefs. How could they have acquired the name "briefs"? The ordinary lawyer requires two lead paragraphs just to inform you that presently he will have something to say further down the page. Naturally, such gobbledygook lends itself to caricature, and the noise of legal writing becomes the stuff of comic strips.

Recently Howland Owl (who seems to be the *Pogo* character most involved in language) ran across an article on rapid reading in a magazine belonging to Miss Sis Boombah. The name of the magazine was *Cultural Sports*, and it said that its

piece could be read by the trained eye in two seconds flat. The Owl read it aloud to Churchy La Femme: "Well, it seems this li'l girl waif put her nose tothewindowan'wasstarvin'todeathan' bzz zip zip zat HOWEVER zz zip swishwhosszhip zap zap zap wap wap BAM BAM BAM."

That hodgepodge is not a caricature of actual noise so much as it is intended to be a revelation of

...man tries to swallow meaning whole as a dog would eat his dinner....

the electric impulses running wild in the mind as a man tries to swallow meaning whole as a dog would eat his dinner.

Children seem instinctively to use the noise which is handiest to convey meaning. Perhaps the child rather than the academician is master in the use of the language. Who is to say which form has the most immediate impact: bring, brought, brought, or bring, brang, brung? Not very many children have to have the latter form pointed out to them; they gravitate toward it. Not laziness but ease of comprehension may be the impulse. The practitioner and not the historian may be the real authority when it comes to actual usage.

The young, or carefree, users of language enjoy new and strange words in much the same manner that adults read with pleasure a Sid Perelman essay employing a strange, exotic, and insanely appropriate vocabulary. As he delights us by throwing caution to the winds, so does the unusual, even the invented word free the child from inhibition. The child is under fetters as he grows because we feel we must shape him to our own ends, rough-hewn or not. He welcomes relief, and with relief comes delight. The wise child never confuses this delight with escape. Escapism is avoidance, and a child learns through daily bruises that there is no escaping the real.

So, wisely, he accepts relief-delight for what it is, a hearty chuckling hunk of self-indulgence. For him the word "hunk" is better than "bit," partly because it has more muscle in its sound and partly because it is a break with the proper. He is sick to death of the proper. Later, lamentably, he will lose his grip on childish things and get relief from the proper through dirty jokes. (It is interesting that some of the greatest wits and humorists have abhorred the dirty joke. This is not out of prudery so much as out of boredom. The unexpected brings a laugh, and to the trained joke mechanic a dirty joke payoff is never unexpected.)

As an illustration of what sort of laughter is most sure for the working comic strip cartoonist or other so-called humorist-writer, consider the Christmas tree. Most children laugh when they first see one. They are at an age when things have been getting steadily duller. They are being trained in various primitive fields of accomplishment, and the humdrum of eating and sleeping has begun to weigh heavily on them. Then at last

"Timmy's dog had a blueberry on his nose!"

there is a break with routine. There's a tree all dressed for Sunday. Result: laughter. This laughter springs from delight, just as it springs from wit or humor, which provide delight or a break with routine.

Too often the sanitary minds of the educational fraternity, being proper, are properly not interested in laughs. Yet the laugh hooks the audience or the reader. When an educator is interested in a laugh, he performs in the manner of a German clown, using exclamation points to denote a so-called surprising fact or observation. Exclamation points should be legally consigned to comic strips and certain news headlines. Children's books should be out of bounds. The news "Timmy's dog had a blueberry on his nose!" is not exactly stop-press information. If it is used at all in a child's book, it should rely on its own strength to drive the child reader into paroxysms of astonishment. Using the exclamation point is like wearing padded shoulders.

People who rely on the exclamation point are playing intellectual squat tag with the child. He expects more from human beings who are supposed to be grown-ups. If the humorist or writer wants to engage the attention of the child, he has to use funny words and devices that the child considers honest.

Children, like most primitive people, make diminutives out of simple nouns, possibly to make the object named more familiar and less alien. Doing this, they sometimes put an -ee ending on "dog" or "Mom," but they also double the use of the noun — "car car," for example. But mothers of the world must face the fact that any adult who goes around saying, "We went to our potty-potty, weren't we good?" will be regarded by one and all as an idiot. It is better not to talk that way; it just destroys the faith of children in their elders.

A certain few adults who happily recalled that they once were children have written books from time to time using words or inventing words which are the delight of children. Lewis Carroll was always honest with his invented words; Edward Lear was a little complicated and sometimes cute, but his inventions were funny and did the job. Beatrix Potter invented ladylike expressions, but they were good on the whole and did not insult the child's intelligence.

Today, aside from the regular comic strip artists, we have one gifted man who makes funny drawings and invents funny words for a living. Dr. Seuss, Ted Geisel, is a solid performer. The child gets no pap from this doctor. When he invents a word, it is funny, short, and serviceable in many emergencies. Ying and Gox and Voom are something a child can grasp. Much better than "putty-tat." Too many made-up words are, in the English schoolboy phrase, just a little wet.

Mother Goose probably should receive a little credit for being a storehouse of invented words most of them intended to be funny. But much of Mother Goose is a file of folk expressions, and time, not being the wisest of editors, has merely knocked off the corners. This has often made round stones out of what may have once been square-cut gems.

Over the past thirty-five years or so the animated cartoon industry has contributed mightily to the supply of noise words. The musical sound track made it possible for all sorts of noises to be used in the many crashes, falls, and splashes with which the ordinary animated cartoon film is studded. In order to define these noises before the picture was shot, storyboard men took to making up their words to denote the various calamities. The storyboard artist works as if he were drawing

KA-PLATZ!

If a horse falls out of a window, he is probably going to make a noise.

a huge comic strip. The action develops panel by panel on a huge wallboard through more or less rough sketches. If a horse falls out of a window, he is probably going to make a noise. Naturally, the artist would spell this noise "krumpf!", or possibly "blamp!" This practice of using noise words of one's own invention spread to comic strip and comic book artists, many of whom had at one time or another worked in animated cartoon studios.

For some reason the classic noise for hitting a friend on the head became "boing!" If you ask the nearest child, he will pronounce it for you, the public having become privy to the information through TV reruns. It is a combination sound coming out of a pig's oink and the unfurling of a tightly wound spring. Very effective.

Some of us have from time to time tried to break away from too close an observance of the rule. Harrison Cady, who drew the *Peter Rabbit* strip for many years, used a device that I always admired, although I was not strictly a Peter Rabbit fan. When a rabbit ran, little words followed his footsteps. They were "run, run, run." If a bug rolled down a hill, the words were "roll, roll, roll."

It must be admitted that this was inspired noise-word making, inasmuch as it depended on the word of the action and was, as far as I know, the only funny thing about Peter Rabbit. The idea, however, led me to experiment at one time

with noise words. Rather than using an unimaginative "pflomp!" I decided that if a fellow fell on his head, the noise might be "Charlie!", or if he was playing a horn, the noise coming out of the bell would be "Schenectady!" Things like that merely puzzled the children and infuriated people named Charlie living in Schenectady. I realized that instead of going to the extreme of playing a condescending game of squat tag with my readers, I was going to the other extreme and was acting with a callous sophistication. True, I was tired of "pflomp!", but the children were still amused by it, and, what is better, they understood it. It is hard to go around with every comic strip or book and explain why the noise "Terre Haute" comes ringing out of a shotgun. Fortunately, the device never became a real trend, and comics were saved.

Children were the ones who put into vocal action

the staccato of an automatic rifle. No sound-effects man or cartoonist was called in. They had to make a noise, and so they made it, using the rapidly opening and closing glottal stop, thus making a gladsome intimidating noise not heard since the last Sumerian drove his last bargain.

Parents always object to such exercises, which break into the funereal quiet of the class-A or TV-less home. All these adults would be enchanted by the babble, chatter, and sheer shrill of the Damascus bazaar, but that is in another country and has charm. At home the poor kid never learns any language except parlor prosaic. Thus, for relief we have the street and the cartoon.

In order to accommodate the taste of the young for something colorful just short of the pool hall, cartoonists have long used swearword substitutes. If somebody annoys Albert, the Alligator, he does not hesitate to say, "Dagnab that backslaggin' dogboned old basket!", which can be translated any way you'd like, according to size and taste.

Frank Willard was a great freehanded cartoonist who, until his death, drew *Moon Mullins*. He would have his men, largely raffish street-corner types of about the early-twenties era, take a drink at the corner saloon and use expressions just short of profanity. One that we can reprint here was "Holy H. Smoke!" The child mind taking this in recognizes it for a paraphrase of the name of one of the Trinity into whose name the freewheeling talkers sometimes place an initial while dealing rather loosely with colorful language. *Moon Mullins* was an honest strip that attracted and held child readers, partly because of its honesty in using language.

So it is that the *Pogo* strip attempts something honest when it has a sorely wounded member scream "rowrbazzle!" This is an unlikely noise in an unlikely strip and therefore likely. The main thing to keep in mind is not to have a word used in an improper setting. Peanuts could holler "rowrbazzle!", upon payment of royalties, and get away with it, but, again, Steve Canyon would have trouble.

"Peanut butter" is a phrase that everybody understands at an early age. You can change it to "peaner buckle" without fear of losing flavor or comprehension. The term "caterpillar," without question, is made to be converted into several things; "caterpiggle" was one I used one time and was deluged with fan mail. One of my sons still uses an invention of his own; it is "callerpitter," which gets the idea across, but he hasn't received any fan mail to speak of.

It occurred to me one year that everybody was talkin' 'bout Christmas but nobody was goin' there. The radio-TV sandblast of carols for commercial purposes grated not only the ear but the sensitivities. So about 1949 I had the characters parody a carol. The attempt was to parody the use of carols, but even though this was a poke at the usage, it was chancy. Readers make mistakes sometimes and think you're making fun of something else besides the real object. It's a risky business. So the choice of carol had to be rather cool. It was discovered finally that one of the few songs used as a carol that had no sacred connotations was "Deck the Halls With Boughs of Holly."

A few of the *Pogo* carolers got together and did a straight parody of the sounds made when you sing the right words to the carol. It came out:

> Oh, deck us all with Boston Charlie,
>   Walla Walla, Wash., and Kalamazoo!
> Nora's freezin' on the trolley . . .
>   Swaller dollar, cauliflower, alley-ga-roo!

This caught on with a number of elderly child minds, and finally children themselves. There was relief in it, and few feelings were bruised. Those who protested against this violation of all that was holy were told as gently as possible that the carol in question was one that was left over from the midwinter pre-Christian pagan rites celebrating the return of the long day in ancient Britain.

Usage of this kind, plus varying type faces, is probably more acceptable in comic strip form than in any other form, and so the *Pogo* strip violates a lot of rules, but the readers seem to enjoy the violations. There is nothing particularly brilliant about the different concoctions of sounds, type faces, and languages; it is just that in the ordinary business of being involved daily with the public, too few writers or cartoonists seem to think it worthwhile to try something unusual. I think it is worthwhile. It saves you from having to be clever at times. As I say, it's a little like wearing a lampshade at the party.

One of the most popular features of this series of Pogo trade paperbacks is the first-ever chronological reprinting of Pogo daily strips. Correspondence from readers supports the joy of reading pure Pogo in sequence as it originally appeared in newspapers. This book features the 1952 daily Pogo strips. Earlier sequential daily strips have been published in: The Best of Pogo (1982), Pogo Even Better (1984), and Outrageously Pogo (1985), all still available at bookstores.

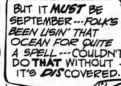

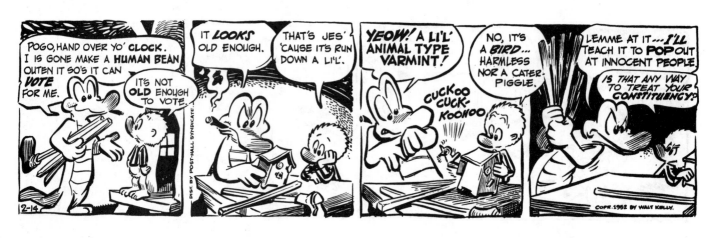

YOU KNOW, TO BUILD *THOUSANDS* OF LI'L' HUMAN BEANS AN' MAKE *VOTERS* OF 'EM WILL BE QUITE A JOB.

SO, PORKYPINE MIGHT BE *RIGHT.* IT MIGHT BE JUST AS WELL TO BUILD A *CANDIDATE,* TOO....

BUT I HAD MY HEART SET ON BEIN' YO' *MILITARY AIDE.*

IF WE DOES THE RIGHT JOB ON THE CANDIDATE, HE'LL *INVITE* YOU TO THE EXECUTIVE MANSION.

SURE, HE COULD WRITE ME A LETTER ON EXECUTIVE TYPE PAPER AN'...

WAIT! WAIT! THE REASON I IS GOIN' EASY ON BUILDIN' *VOTERS* IS WE'LL HAFTA TEACH 'EM TO READ AN' WRITE 'CAUSE VOTERS REALLY *GOTTA*...BUT WITH A *CANDIDATE* IT MOUGHT BE *DIFFERENT;* MEBBE WE CAN SNEAK BY AN'...

HE COULD AT LEAST GIMME A 'PHONE CALL.

2-26 COPR. 1952 WALT KELLY   DIST. BY POST-HALL SYNDICATE, INC.

OWL, IF YOU AN' ALBERT IS BUILDIN' A *MACHINE CANDIDATE,* YOU CAN USE THIS OL' GRAN'DADDY CLOCK OF MINE.

DANDY! JES' *JAMES DANDY.*

2-27 DIST. BY POST-HALL SYNDICATE, INC.

CUCKOO! CUCKOO! FOUR-SEVENTY-FIVE AND *ALL IS WELL!*

WHOO! HE DON'T EVEN KNOW WHAT TIME IT IS.

IT'S *SATURDAY,* BRIGHT EYES! WANNA MAKE SOMETHIN' OUT OF IT?!

YES. MAKE IT WEDNESDAY AND I'LL SETTLE FOR THAT FOUR SEVENTY-FIVE.

WHO'S THE *AUTHORITARY* ON THIS STUFF? *ME* OR THAT *GOOSLYMUSH?*

I DUNNO, POGO, YOU THINK I CAN MAKE A CANDIDATE OUTEN A CLOCK WHAT GOT A RABBIT FOR A CUCKOO?

WHY NOT?

COPR. 1952 WALT KELLY

THINK THIS OUGHT TO HAVE A MUSTACHE LIKE *GROVER?*

OWL IS BUILDIN' A MACHINE CANDIDATE.

HOW FEARSOMELY *DROLL.*

2-28   DIST. BY POST-HALL SYNDICATE, INC.

EIGHTY-FOUR O'CLOCK! *CUCKOO-HOO!* WEATHER FORECAST: RAIN AND...

CAN'T YOU CONTAIN YOURSELF 'TIL *EASTER?* YOU'RE ONLY SPOSED TO STRIKE ON THE *HOUR.*

FOOF!

BY JING, IF YOU GET FANCY WITH *ME,* I'LL STRIKE EVERY *FIFTEEN* MINUTES AND I'LL PULL OUT EVERY CUCKOO 'TWEEN HERE AN' *CAP-ITOL HILL.*

DON'T ROUSE ORGANIZED TYPES.

COPR. 1952 WALT KELLY

WHAT D'YA MEAN, TODAY IS FEBR'ARY? IT'S MARCH!

Y'KNOW, IT *IS* THE 29TH OF FEBRUARY.

AN' *HERE* COMES THE *BEAVER GIRL PATROL.*

NO.... IT'S LEAP DAY.

2-29 DIST. BY POST-HALL SYNDICATE, INC.   COPR. 1952 WALT KELLY

THOUGHT I HEERD *MEN-TYPE VOICES,* SIS.

KEEP YO' EYE PEELT.

CUCKOO RICKY TICKY TICKEY TONK
TOCK
TICK TICK
CUKKOO DING DING TOCK TOCK
TICKETY TOCK A TOOK A TICK
OH TICK OH TOCKTOR

WELL, LET'S LEAP ALONG, SISTER.....UNLESS...HEE HEE YOU WANTS TO *PREE* POSE TO A CLOCK.

HEAD FOR RUSSIA, EVERY DAY IS LADIES DAY IN *PRAVDA.*

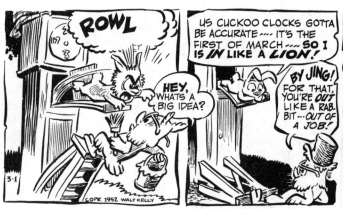

QUICK, *QUICK!* MIZ BEAVER, THE ROOKERY MOTHER OF THE BOY BIRD-WATCHERS IS FAINTED.

4-3
DIST. BY
POST-HALL
SYNDICATE

I'LL *REE*-VIVE HER WITH THE WATER IN THE BUCKET.

AWAKE! AWAKE --- FOR DAWN WHICH SCATTERED --- OOP!

SPLAMP!

I ADMITS I FERGOT TO *REE*-MOVE THEM FISH FROM THE BAIT-BUCKET BUT THAT *CRAWFISH* GITTIN' IN ON IT WAS HIS *OWN* IDEA.

FOO, A BEAUTIFUL GAL WASTES HER TIME GRACIN' UP *THIS* SWAMP.

COPR. 1952 WALT KELLY.

US *BATS* ISN'T GOT A *LEADER* NOW WE LOST OUR *PANTS.* MIZ BEAVER *FAINTS* AN' DEACON DISAPPROVES.

4-4
DIST. BY
POST-HALL
SYNDICATE

'LONG AS YOU BOY BIRDWATCHERS IS HARD UP FOR A LEADER, I'LL SLIP INTO UNIFORM AN' LEAD A LI'L FIELD TRIP.

WE ISN'T *THAT* HARD UP.

Albert

NOW *OFF* WE GO MEN.

WE'RE *OFF* ALL RIGHT.

COPR. 1952 WALT KELLY.

JUST WHAT I'M LOOKIN' FOR! A CHIMNEY.

HMM?

A STORK! A *STORK!* A SIGN OF GOOD LUCK

IF YOU IS A LUCKY STORK, WHY DOES YOU PICK *ME* TO NEST ON?

PLEASE TILT THE CHIMNEY UPRIGHT AN' *STOP* COM-PLAININ'.

OH BOY! THIS *IS* A LUCKY SIGN.

DIST. BY
POST-HALL
SYNDICATE 4-5

JUST HOLD THAT WHILST I GOES FORTH FER STICKS AN' STUFF.

WHILE HE IS PICKIN' UP *TRASH* I IS HIKIN' TO LAPLAND.

WHOA! YOU IS COURTIN' *DEE*-SASTER.

COPR. 1952 WALT KELLY.

A STORK NESTIN' ON YO' CHIMNEY IS *LUCKY.* BUT CHASIN' HIM OFF IS *SURE DEATH.*

OR *WORSE*

THINK IT OVER AN' KEEP YO' FLUE OPEN.

AS ROOKERY-MOTHER TO YOU *BOY BIRD WATCHERS,* I DE-MANDS YOU FINDS YO' PANTS AN'-- *SAY,* WHAT AILS OL' GLOOMY-GLUM?

LAW! LOOKS LIKE HE GOT A CASE OF THE FRITTURS --- WELL, I CAN'T DO *ALL* TH' BIRD-GAZIN' MYSELF..

HE IS FALLED INTO GOOD LUCK.

4-7
DIST. BY
POST-HALL
SYNDICATE

WELL, WE IS DOIN' *OUR* PART, WE IS WATCHIN' A BIRD RIGHT NOW ----- OL' STORK!

ORK!

WHAT'S-A-MATTER WITH THE FAT OLD PARTY? SHE RUN OFF WHEN SHE SEE ME COMIN' IN WITH A LOAD OF STICKS FER THE NEST.

COPYRIGHT 1952 BY WALT KELLY

WELL, I GUESS *WE* WON'T BE VOTIN' FOR POGO!

GONNA WRITE IN YOUR OWN SELFS?

'COURSE NOT! IT WOULDN'T BE FAIR TO PRECIPITATE A LANDSLIDE. *BUT POGO'S CAMPAIGN MANAGER* IS HAD IT PROVED TO HIM THAT THERE'S A GROUND SWELL OF OPINION AGAINST POGO.

HOW PROVED?

HE GOT UP TO SPEAK FOR THE CANDIDATE AN' GOT *THROWN AT WITH EGGS!* THAT SHOWS POGO IS *WASHED UP.* THE *PUBLIC* IS *SPOKE!* *FAIR* MINDED AN' *SQUARE* ... UH-M

-- HEADED?

WELL, BULLY FOR *YOU,* BOYS. KEEP FINGERIN' THE PULSE OF THE GRASS ROOTS ... *BUT TRY TO HOLD OFF WRITIN' IN YOUR OWN NAMES.* IT'LL BE TOUGH BECAUSE CONSTANT PROOF OF OTHER CANDIDATES' CRIMINAL WAYS WILL ARISE ...

US'LL BE FIRM AN' REFRAIN 'CAUSE IT WOULDN'T BE SPORTIN'...

THRU ELECTION DAY?

COPR. 1992 WALT KELLY

YOU CAN STOP MAKIN' THEM *MACHINE* VOTERS ..... IT'S TIME WE WAS ALL BEIN' *GOOD FRIENDS* WITH P.T. BRIDGEPORT.

WHAT?

5-12 - DIST. BY POST-HALL SYNDICATE.

WHY, THAT BIG OL' *BLOWHEAD!* HE'S A REAL *FIRST OF MAY* CIRCUS CIPHER ... A *RUBE* IN *DISGUISE* ... A SAWDUST FOGHORN ... WHAT'S HE GOT TO BE FRIENDS WITH?

MM

A BIG BAG OF MONEY.

TO P.T. BRIDGEPORT

LEMME HELP YOU CARRY THAT TO THE DEAR *DEAR* OLD PARTY! WHO'S SENDIN' THIS *DIRTY* OLD MONEY TO THE *SWEET EVER-LOVIN'* CHAP? HE'S GONE NEED A HAND *COUNTIN'* IT.

STOP SHOVIN' AIN'T NO SPECIAL DEE-LIVERY STAMP ON IT.

COPR 1862 WALT KELLY.

LET'S JES' *LOOK* AT THE MONEY WHAT BEEN SENT TO P.T. BRIDGEPORT ... HE WON'T MISSALI'L'BIT IF WE -- HEEHOOHAHA

STOP *THAT!* THIS MAIL MIGHT BE *FOURTH CLASS* BUT --

5-13 U.S. 4th A

THE BAG *COULD* OF BEEN DAMAGED IN *TRANSIT.*

HEEHEEHO HOHOOHA HAHOHEE!

I HAD A FRIEND TRIED THAT ONCE AN' HE WOUND UP IN THE *BIG ARENA* PLAYIN' A *20 YEAR* GAME OF *ROCK HOCKEY.*

DIST. BY POST-HALL SYNDICATE.

20 YEARS?

THE KIND OF *GIDDY* FRIENDS *YOU* HAVE, PROB'LY NEED LESSONS LIKE THAT ..... *CHUG-CHUG, STOP HOLDIN' US UP!* GIT GOIN' FOR P.T. BRIDGEPORT'S PLACE.

HOLD UP! IT'S AGIN *REG-ULATIONS* TO RUSH *FOURTH CLASS MAIL.*

COPR 1952 WALT KELLY

DON'T FERGIT TO REMIND P.T. NOW, THAT THIS BAG OF *MONEY* WAS HEAVY AN' HE COULD SHOW HIS APPRECIATION BY-- HEEHO HAHOHEEHAHEE

5-14 U.S. 4th A MAIL

DIST. BY POST-HALL SYNDICATE.

WE WAS WONDERIN', MR. BRIDGEPORT, (SEEIN' AS WE BRUNG THAT BAGFUL) IF WE COULD DIP IN AN' -- AW HAW HEE HOO HAHA HA --

A REASONABLE REQUEST! *TAKE ALL YOU WISH!*

WOW ALL?

OF *COURSE, OWL! HELP YOUR'SELF TO BUTTONS!*

BUTTONS?

AYE -- AREN'T THEY BEAUTIES? FOR ☞ POGO BUTTONS ☜ HIS CANDIDATURE EMBLAZONED ☰I GO POGO!

COPR. 1952 WALT KELLY

GOSH, MIZ MAM'SELLE, *EVER'BODY* LEFT FOR THE **CON**VENTION 'CEPT ME.! *I* OVERSLEPT.

AN' *ME*.... I WAS OCCUPY MAKING THE PICKLE-JAM

PERHAP YOU LIKE ENJOY PICKLE-JAM? IN SO FARS AS WE ARE *ALONE* IN SWAMP -----

ALONE?

CHICAGO IS ONLY A SLEEPER JUMP AWAY AN' *I* IS AS GOOD A SLEEPER AS *ANY*!

SO...

HE DOES NO LIKE PICKLE-JAM.

POGO WILL KNOW WHAT WE IS FORGOT

SMOKE FILLED ROOM

ASK **POGO** WHAT IT IS WE'S FORGOT TO TAKE TO THE **CONVENTION**.

HE'S BACK *AFT*.

RUSTLE UP *POGO*

THE ORANGE

7·7 DIST. BY POST-HALL SYNDICATE.

HE'S ASTERN. *US'LL* HAVE HIM QUERIED ON THE SUBJECT.

P.T., FIND OUT FROM **POGO** BACK THERE *WHAT IT IS* *WE* IS LEFT BEHIND.

AYE, *Throcksodden,* MY BOY, STEP AFT AND *question the* GOOD ← CANDIDATE →

AFT? THIS IS AS *AFTER* AS WE GO.

WHERE *IS* THE CANDIDATE? WE GOTTA ASK HIM WHAT WE FORGOT TO TAKE TO THE **CONVENTION**.

POGO IS *NO-WHERES* TO BE FOUND.

NOWHERES TO BE FOUND? WELL ---- UM---- IN **THAT CASE,** WE DON'T NEED TO ASK HIM.

YOU REMEMBERS WHAT US IS *FORGOT?* *WHAT* WHAT?

COPR. 1962 WALT KELLY

7·8 DIST. BY POST-HALL SYNDICATE

THE CANDIDATE.

GOSH, THAT'S A *REE-LIEF!* IF *YOU* HADN'T RE-MEMBERED, WE'D OF BEEN *LOOKIN'* AND *LOOKIN'* FOR HIM ----

---TO ASK *HIM* WHAT WE *FOR-GOT* AND WE *COULDN'T* OF FOUND HIM IF WE FORGOT HIM AND, IF WE COULDN'T *ASK* HIM, WE MIGHT NEVER HAVE *KNOWED* WE FORGOT HIM.

THIS LOOKS LIKE THE PLACE, MEN.

7·9 DIST. BY POST-HALL SYNDICATE

HURRY, BOYS. WE'RE GONNA SLIDE THE DOOR **SHUT.**

ALLRIGHT NOW, MEN, WE GOTTA PICK A *PRESIDENT* FOR THE **MOUSE UNION** OF THE *U.S.* AND *A,* LOCAL 25, SWAMP DISTRICT.

CHICAGO

COPR. 1952 WALT KELLY

Strip 1 (7-15):

UNEASY LIES THE HEAD WHAT SLEEPS ON A *RAIL-ROAD TRACK*....

I DUNNO.... IT'S KINDA COOL ON THE HEAD BONE.

WELL, IT'S A YEAR WHEN US NEEDS COOL HEADS AN' THIS WAY THEY'D BE ALL OVER *EVERYWHERE*.

ANYWAYS ONLY *SLOW* FREIGHTS GOES THRU HERE.

HAUL IN YO' *SKULL* --- *HERE* COME A FREIGHT *NOW* .... SEE HER LIGHT?

KINDA SMALL AIN'T IT? AN' *NO CHOO CHOO*.

OH--- H'LO MR. GLOW-WORM. BACK FROM *CHICAGO*?

YEP.... I DON'T CARE *WHAT* THEY SAY OUT THERE... I *STILL GLOW PLOGLO*.

7-15 DIST. BY POST HALL SYNDICATE.

COPR. 1952 WALT KELLY

Strip 2 (7-16):

DIN'T YOU HAVE A OL' *NUNKLE*, NAME OF *PIERCE*, IN CHICAGO, PORKYPINE?

YEP, HE *ALLUS* SAID, "THIS OLD WORLD 'UD BE *O-KAY* IF IT WERE ONLY PEOPLED WITH *ME*."

HE ALSO SAID, "LIVE EVERY DAY AS IF IT WAS *NEXT TO YOUR LAST*."

A *NO* BLOBLE SENTIMINTS.

TROUBLE *IS*.... HE *NEVER* CLEARED UP WHICH "NEXT" DAY HE HAD IN MIND...

--- THE ONE *NEXT BEFORE* OR THE ONE *NEXT AFTER* YOUR LAST.

7-16 DIST. BY POST-HALL SYNDICATE.

COPR. 1952 WALT KELLY

Strip 3 (7-17):

WHAT WAS YOUR OBJECTION TO THE *FIRST* CONVENTION, POGO?

MMM~~

WELL, IT WAS *STUFFY* AN' *CROWDED* AN' *EVER'*BODY HAD *HORNS* AN' HOLLERED. -----

HORNS? WHAT DID THEY *HOLLER*..?

MOSTLY "*MOO*".

YOU GOT INTO THE *WRONG* CONVENTION, SON ----- *THAT* WAS THE STOCKYARD CROWD.

WELL .... *THEY'LL* NEVER WIN IN A BREEZE.

7-17 DIST. BY POST-HALL SYNDICATE.

COPR. 1952 WALT KELLY

Strip 4 (7-18):

I CAN GIT *YOU* TWO INTO THE MOUSE *CONVENTION* 'CAUSE YOU IS RATTY LOOKIN'.

ENTER, *UNION* MEMBER.

I GOT TWO *THROWBACKS* WITH ME.

THESE MICE IS GOT SNAPPY LI'L' TRAPS.

FROM EATIN' SHARP CHEESE.

NOW, BEFORE WE HAVE NOMINATIONS, WE GOT HERE *THREE* COMPLAINTS FROM SEVERAL *BLIND MICE*... SEEMS A FARMER'S WIFE CUT OFF THEIR TAILS WITH A *CARVIN' KNIFE*.

THIS IS *A-GIN* WORK RULE 765B. SO WHAT DOES THE MEMBERSHIP *PREE-POSE*?

I, SQUEAK, MOVES THEY ALL GITS *SEVERANCE PAY*.

I SQUEAKS THE MOTION.

SQUEAK.

SQUEAK.

7-18 DIST. BY POST-HALL SYNDICATE.

COPR. 1952 WALT KELLY

YOU MADE A *BIG HIT* WITH THE *MOUSE UNION* YESTERDAY, ALBERT. LEMME *INNERDUCE* YOU AS POGO'S MILITARY AIDE.

MEMBERS OF THE CONVENTION, IF YOU ALL WILL ASSUME *ATTITUDES* OF *QUIETUDE*, I WOULD LIKE TO PRESENT A *IMMINENT* MILITARY FIGURE, A MAN WHO--

GOOD! OUR UNION GOT QUESTIONS FOR A MILITARY MAN..... WE IS IN FAVOR OF *SLASHIN'* THE MILITARY AID.... WE WOULD *CUT* ANY MILITARY AID TO THE *BONE!*

AL-*BERT!* YOU COME *BACK* HERE.

7-19 DIST. BY POST-HALL SYNDICATE.

OL' *HOUN'* DOG IS MAKIN' THE *KEYNOTE SPEECH* TO THE MICE 'CAUSE HE HATES CATS TOO.

IN THE INT'REST OF PARTY HARMONY I WON'T EXPRESS MY OPINIONS.

OL' *DOG* WILL SPEAK OUT *HIS* OPINIONS THO', ALL COMPLIMENTABLE TO *DOGS* ----

TO BE *FAIR*, HE IS MORE FOR *MICE* THAN FOR *CATS*.

'CAUSE HE THINKS *MICE* ARE JES' *LI'L* SIZED *DOGS*.

7-21

I FEEL THE *CONVENTION* DESERVES A CLEAR CUT HONEST STATEMENT ON HOW THE *DOG, MAN'S BEST FRIEND,* VIEWS THE *ISSUES*..... TO THIS END I HAVE LEFT *NO STONE* UNTURNED.

TURNED OVER YOUR *MIND*, HUH?

HERE COMES MY *SPEECH* NOW ----*IT PROVES MY MIND IS MINE OWN!*

AN' WELCOME TO IT, TOO.

I HAD TROUBLE SPELLIN' *NOBLE CANINE.*

DOG IS GONE SQUEAK BY.

PZZT.... IS YOU WROTE MY *KEYNOTE* SPEECH?

YEP..... IT'S A *PROTEST* AGIN EVER'THING.

7-22

AH, THE UNMITIGATED GALL IS SPLIT INTO THREE PARTS! GREED, CRUELTY AND *STEW-PIDDITTY!* A *POX* ON THE USURY OF ANY PARTY WHO ASKS THE POUND OF FLESH.

DIST. BY POST-HALL SYND.

TIME WILL TELL WHO ARE THE *REAL PEOPLE*... THE MISERABLE SUM OF *77¢* WILL NOT BREAK *ME* -- BUT THE *FLINTY HEART* WILL QUAIL ---AND THE ETERNAL COLLECTION OF ---

GIMME! YOU IS READIN' A LETTER I WAS WRITIN' TO A 1930 CREDITOR IN KEOKUK.

WELL, *GOL*-DERN. IT SEEMED LIKE A *EXCELLENT* SUMMARY OF *PARTY* SENTIMINTS.

COPR 1952 WALT KELLY

IN THESE DAYS WE *NEED* A LEADER, A *FEARLESS* HELMSMAN, A *MAN* ADMIRED BY *DOGS*, FOR THE NOBLE *DOG* IS A GREAT JUDGE OF THE HAND ON THE *END* OF THE LEASH.

7-23 DIST. POST-HALL SYNDICATE

INASMUCH AS *DOGS* ARE MEN'S BEST FRIENDS, I SPEAK FOR A MAN WELL KNOWN AND *LOVED*... A MAN WHO I STAND BEHIND, A MAN WHO STANDS BEHIND *ME*; A *MAN WHO STANDS BEHIND YOU*..

COPR 1952 WALT KELLY

A MAN *YOU* STANDS BEHIND ---- I GIVES YOU A MAN WHO -- WHO -- UH -- I GIVES YOU A WHO A MAN I -- UM -- WHO -- UH *GIVES* YOU A MAN --- WHO GIVES -- A MAN WHO -- WHO ?

I FERGITS WHO THE MAN WHO.

IT DON'T MATTER. *NOBODY* IS LEFT TO *INNARDUCE* HIM TO.

CAN'T GIT ON HOME ... GOTTA HAVE MY *HAT*.

HURRY UP WITH YO'R *BOATIN'* PARTY, YOU BUGS.

HEY, MR. PORKYPINE! YOU SAY YOU WASHES YO' BACK ON THE *IN-SIDE* SO YOU DON'T GIT STUCK ... HOW'S YOU GIT YO' *OUT-SIDE* SKIN CLEAN?

YEAH?!

WELL, I TURNS MYSELF *INSIDE OUT* AN' THAT PUTS THE INSIDE OUTSIDE SO I GITS OFFSIDE THE DOWNSIDE AN'---

HOLD IT! US'LL GIVE YO' THE HAT BACK. E-NUFF IS *EE-NUFF!*

8-16 DIST. BY POST HALL SYNDICATE.

COPR. 1952 WALT KELLY.

MIZ MAM'SELLE HEPZIBAH GOT ME STOOPED OVER IN A *STOOPID* POSITION FROM BEIN' *STARCHED STIFF!*

SHE GIMME A BOOK IN *FRENCH.*

IT TELLS HOW TO *UNSTIFF* THE *STARCH* OUTEN YOU SO'S YOU KIN *STRAIGHTEN UP!*

KIN *YOU* READ FRENCH?

HARD TO SAY... I NEVER TRIED. *DAGNAG* THIS RAGBAGGY OL' *BLAGGARDIN'*...

DON'T LOSE YO' TEMPER JES 'CAUSE IT'S *HARD.*

'TAIN'T *THAT!* THIS BUG KEEPS RUNNIN' 'ROUN', DOTTIN' EYES, CROSTIN' TEES AN' MESSIN' UP THE *TRANSU-LATION.*

VIVE LE MOT

8-18 DIST. BY POST-HALL SYNDICATE, INC.

COPR 1952 WALT KELLY

IN AN SMUCH AS MAM'SELLE MIZ *HEP-ZIBAH* GOT YOU STARCHED INTO THAT POSE, SHE GIMME A *FRENCH* BOOK WHAT TELLS HOW TO *UNSTARCH* A OWL.

DON'T BLEEVE YOU KIN READ IT.

WHY, *CERTIMENTLY* I KIN READ IT.... *LIKE IT WAS* ENGLISH

BE BETTER IF YOU READS IT LIKE IT WAS *FRENCH.*

I MEANS I READS FRENCH AS GOOD AS I READS ENGLISH!

A BITTER BLOW! I IS *HEERD* YOU READ ENGLISH.

JES' FER *THAT*, I'M GONE *LEAVE* YOU STIFF! BUT, TO PROVE I *KNOW* FRENCH, I'LL RECITE ALL OF *HICKORY-DICKORY PARLEE-VOO.*

YOU BETTER DO IT ON YO' *OWN TIME,* OR YOU IS GONE BE LOOKIN' FOR A JOB IN ANOTHER COMIC STRIP.

DIST. BY POST HALL SYNDICATE, INC.

8-19

1952 COPR. WALT KELLY

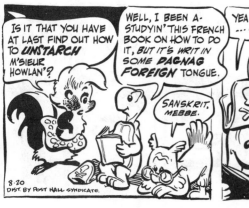

IS IT THAT YOU HAVE AT LAST FIND OUT HOW TO *UNSTARCH* M'SIEUR HOWLAN'?

WELL, I BEEN A-STUDYIN' THIS FRENCH BOOK ON HOW TO DO IT, BUT IT'S WRIT IN SOME *DAGNAG* FOREIGN TONGUE.

SANSKRIT, MEBBE.

YEAH... *SAMSKRIMPS* ...SEE?

BUT, HERE IS NOT *FOREIGN TONGUE*....IS MERELY AN' POSITIVE *ONLY* FRENCH!

PARDONNY-ME, BUT *I* KNOWS A *MESS* OF FRENCH WORDS... APPLE-MA LA DELUGE, DES MOINES, PIE A LA MODE AN' R.S.V.P......

R.S.V.P. IS *NOT A WORD.*

IT'S *FRENCH*, AIN'T IT? AN' I DON'T *SEE* IT IN THAT THERE *BOOK*, SO HOW COULD...

ALORS! YOU HAVE RIGHT, M'SIEUR ...THEY *LEFT OUT* YOUR WORDS! -- THIS IS, PERHAPS, BOOK *EN FRANCAIS!*

SEE? *SEE? SEE!?*

8-20 DIST. BY POST HALL SYNDICATE.

COPR 1952 WALT KELLY

FRIENDS! WE IS JOINED YOU ---- THE DEACON SENT US OVER TO TELL YOU WE ARE THE *NEW* MEMBERS.

NEW MEMBERS OF *WHAT*? IS THE LOONY BIN GOT TWO *VACANCIES*?

WE'RE *NO LONGER COWBIRDS*----WE SWORE OFF....NOW, PURE IN HEART, WE WISH TO TELL ALL WE KNOW OF THIS *FALSE HEARTED* CANDIDATE, *POGO*!

ONCE A COWBIRD ALWAYS A COWBIRD!

NO! WE'VE *CHANGED!* WE SUDDENLY SAW HOW *VILE* WE'D BEEN WHEN *POGO PROTECTED OUR RIGHTS*----IT TURNED OUR STOMACHS ... HE *DEFENDED* MISER'BLE SWINE SUCH AS WE!

HE SAID WE COULDN'T *HELP* BEIN' COWBIRDS ... *HE* KEPT US FROM BEIN' *BEAT UP* .... THE *SCURVY, SUBVERSIVE SCOUNDREL!*

WHAT A DIRTY INSULT! YOU SHOULD OF PUNCHED HIM RIGHT IN THE EYE.

9-13 DIST. BY POST-HALL SYNDICATE, INC.

COPR. 1952 WALT KELLY.

AH THERE, PORKYPINE, YOU'RE JUST IN TIME TO SEE *POGO*, DISGUISED AS A *ORPHAN GAL*, RUN AWAY FROM HOME.

WHAT'S HE PUTTIN' THAT *EXCELSIOR* ON HIS HEAD FOR?

HE'S GOTTA WEAR A *GOLDY WIG* LIKE THE FUNNY PAPERS SHOW ALL GAL ORPHANS DO. *ALSO I* GITS TO BE THE *FAITHFUL DOG.*

NOTHIN' IS LIKE A FAITHFUL DOG. A FAMBLY IN OREGON GIVE THEIR DOG TO A OL' LADY IN MAINE AN', YOU KNOW, ONE NIGHT THEY HEARS A *SCRATCHIN' AT THE DOOR...* WELL, SIR, -- *IT WAS THE FAITHFUL DOG!*

NO, IT WAS THE OL' LADY CRAWLED *43,000* MILES HER ELBOWS TO ASK 'EM TAKE BACK THE DOG 'CAUSE HE WAS EATEN HER OUTEN HOUSE *AND* HOME.

PHOOMPH.

9-15 DIST. BY POST-HALL SYNDICATE.

COPR. 1952 WALT KELLY

SO YOU IS RUNNIN' OFF DISGUISED AS A *ORPHAN* 'CAUSE P.T. BRIDGEPORT WANTS YOU TO MAKE SPEECHES AN' RUN FOR PRESIDENT?

YEP, AN' *MIZ MÄM'SELLE HEPZIBAH* WANTS TO GIT A FIRST LADY ALL MARRIED UP.

TO *WHOM?*

TO *MEEM.*

YOUM TO *WHOM?*

TO *HERM!*

IS SHE *SEED* YOU *LATELY?*

9-16 DIST. BY POST-HALL SYNDICATE.

COPR. 1952 WALT KELLY

YOU SAY THE Candidate is taking *A Little Trip*!?

YUP, HE WANTS TO GIT AWAY FROM THE HULLA-BALOODLE.

US *PACIFISTS* IS JOINED THE BOY BIRD WATCHERS AN' WE *HEARD* WHAT YOU SAID...... *SO! POGO IS SNEAKING OUT!?*

WE *KNEW* HE WOULDN'T BE ABLE TO FACE THE *TRUTHS* UNFURLED FROM OUR NEWLY CLEANSED HEARTS. *IT WAS HE WHO KEPT US FROM BEING STOMPED WHEN WE WERE TRAITOROUS COWBIRDS*...... WHAT A RECORD OF DUPLICITY!

WELL, IF *YOU* CHANGED, *POGO* MUST OF *TOO.* MAYBE *NOW* HE'D AS SOON YOU *HAD* BEEN KINDA STOMPED OUT---- *NOW* IT'S YOUR NOBLE DUTY TO *DROP DEAD* SO WE CAN *ALL* RELAX.

9-17 DIST. BY POST-HALL SYNDICATE.

COPR. 1952 WALT KELLY

WHACK!

10-2

POOMF!

HOW'RE THINGS GOING OUT HERE FELLOWS?

NO FAIR! HE *NEVER* TOUCHED FIRST!

I *DID TOO!* ALL OVER!

COPR. 1952 WALT KELLY

COULDN'T YOU *LEAVE* FOR A *HAIRCUT* OR GO VISIT YOUR AUNT MOOMY OR *SOMETHING?*

I WAS IN HERE FIRST, *MISTER ABBONER DOUBLEDAY.*

ICE CREAM and UMPIRING NEATLY DONE

10-3
DIST. BY POST-HALL SYNDICATE.

A *POP FOUL!* WHERE'S THE *CATCHER?!*

ICE CREAM and UMPIRING NEATLY DONE

GOT IT!

NO FAIR!

COPR. 1952 WALT KELLY

ICE CREAM and UMPIRING NEATLY DONE

"NO FAIR" IS RIGHT! LOOKY AT WHAT YOU DID TO MY *TUTTI FRUTTI!*

I *NEVER* ATE NONE. JES' SORTA SAT ON IT A LI'L', THERE IN THE COOL.

ICE CREAM UMPIRING

LOOKIN' ALL OVER FOR THAT *LOST BALL.*

AN' LESSEN WE *FINDS* IT, THE 1952 WORLD SERIES IS BUT A *GLORY BLAZONED* PAGE IN THE *GOLDEN BOOK OF SPORT.*

10-4
DIST BY POST-HALL SYNDICATE

I GOT IT! I GOT IT! I GOT IT! I GOT IT I GOT IT I GOT IT I GOT IT I GOT IT.. HEY! *HEY!* I GOT IT..

DOLT! YOU SHOULDA OF *KNEW BETTER!*

I GO

COPR. 1952 WALT KELLY

DOLT IS RIGHT! YOU *SHOULD* OF KNOWED BETTER ---- SEE, IT DON'T SAY "*OFFICIAL NATIONAL LEAGUE BALL*" ON IT NOWHERES!

NOR AMERICAN NUTHER.

NEXT TIME YOU CAN *HARD-BOIL IT!*

PFAFF! DO I LOOK LIKE A PERCOLATOR?

WHAT *HO!*

YOU SAID IT.

10-6
DIST BY POST-HALL SYNDICATE.

HOPE YOU DON'T MIND ME POINTIN' OUT THAT YOU'RE A PECULIAR LOOKIN' CROWD.

YOU'RE A MIGHTY PECULIAR LOOKIN' *CROWD* YOURSELF.

THAT'S *NO* WAY TO TALK TO A MAN *OUT-OF-WORK.*

YOU LOOKIN' FOR A *JOB?*

YEP, I'M A UNEMPLOYED *PRESIDENTIAL CANDIDATE* --- KNOW ANY LOOSE PARTIES NEEDIN' A MAN?

COPR 1952 WALT KELLY

— 74 —

OL' POGO MADE P.T. MAD 'CAUSE HE WOULDN'T USE A READY MADE SPEECH.

FRIENDS, NEIGHBORS AN' COUSINS---

I URGE YOU ALL TO GIT OUT AN' *VOTE*

WE DIN' HEAR ALL YO' SPEECH.... JUST HEARD YOU SAY GIT ON *OUT* AN' *VOTE.*

THAT'S ENOUGH... 'LONG AS YOU DO THAT, YOU *CAN'T* GO WRONG.

BUT WHO FER?

YEAH WHOFER?

SCRATCH ANY CANDIDATE AN' YOU'LL FIND A GOOD AMERICAN BOY!

I AGREES, SOME COULD BE SCRATCHED

SCRATCH ME

COME ON OVER TO YOUR PLACE FOR COOKIES AN' MILK AN' I'LL DRUM YOU UP A CHORUS OF PONY BOY.

COPR. 1952 WALT KELLY

11-4

DIST. BY POST HALL SYNDICATE.

A *VICTORY!* A *VICTORY!* A MORAL *VICTORY!* POGO LOST.

WHO WON?

MMF.... IT'D BEEN BETTER DID *POGO* WIN --- COULD OF SPELT IT OUT EASIER ...THIS NAME GOT *"N" IN IT,* AN' A *"O"* AN' A FEW OF THEM *"E"*S ... GOT *"S"* IN HER, TOO.

"T" TOO?

YESSIR! DON'T MIND IF I *DO!* THIS FELLOW SEEMS LIKE A BOY WHAT WRIT A BOOK ONCE.

OH, THE MAN WHAT GIVED HIS *BIRTHDAY* AWAY TO THE LI'L GAL WHAT WAS BORN ON *CHRISTMAS DAY?*

WELL, *NO!* NOT EXACTLY *HIM...* THE *OTHER* ONE --- AN' HE'S BEEN A *WINNER* BEFORE.

I *ALWAYS* SAID: *CASEY O'STENGEL* WOULD MAKE A *GREAT* PRESIDENT.

COPR. 1952 WALT KELLY

11-5 DIST. BY POST HALL SYNDICATE.

THING FOR POGO TO DO IS KEEP ON RUNNIN' FOR THE NEXT *FOUR* YEARS. COME *1956* HE WILL HAVE PILED UP *E*-NOUGH VOTES TO CARRY *BOTH* THE *NORTH* AN' *SOUTH AMERICAN* COUNTENANCE

11-6

COUNT-ENANCE?

HE MEANS *CONT-INENTS.*

DIST. BY POST HALL SYNDICATE.

JES' WHAT I SAYS ... COUNTENANCE.

I LIKES PEOPLE WHO AIN'T AFEARED TO USE *BIG* WORDS.

COME WHAT MAY.

RIGHT.

COPR. 1952 WALT KELLY

IF YOU GOT NOTHIN' *EXCITIN'* OR *AMAZIN'* PLANNED LIKE THE EVENTS OF THE PAST FEW WEEKS I BELIEVE I'LL VISIT MY UNCLE *BALDWIN* ---

OKAY.

11-7 DIST. BY POST HALL SYNDICATE.

HE IS ALWAYS WORRYIN' ABOUT LOSIN' HIS *HAIR.*

WELL, AT *HIS* AGE, HE AIN'T GOT MUCH ELSE TO DO.

WHOOSH! WHERE'D YOU GIT THE *OUTFIT?*

NONE OF YOUR *NEEDLENOSIN'* BUSINESS.

WAS THAT *YOU?*

DON'T BELIEVE IT *WAS* ..... I AIN'T GOT *NO* HAT LIKE THAT.

COPR. 1952 WALT KELLY

DING BING IT! JES' WHEN A MIGRATORY MAN NEEDS A FISH, IT STARTS TO RAIN! THEM FISH AIN'T GONE BITE NOW... GIT HAULED OUT AN' GIT ALL WET.

THEY'S DOWN BELOW SITTIN' ROUN' THE FIRE TELLIN' LIES 'BOUT THE BIG FISHERMENS WHO ALMOST CAUGHT 'EM---- AN' I AIN'T GONE SIT OUTSIDE HERE----

---GITTIN' SOAKED TO THE SKIN OFFERIN' UNREQUITED LOVE TO A MESS OF INDOOR, UNSPORTIN', SUMMER SOLDIERIN', SEDENTARY, PISCATORY PUSSY FOOTERS! THEY KIN DIG THEIR OWN WORMS.

AIN'T NO USE KEEPIN' YOU FELLAS AWAY FROM YO' FAM'LIES.

FISH AIN'T BITIN' NOHOW IN THIS RAIN---AN' IF I GITS ANY HUNGRIER, IT AIN'T GONE PAY YOU TO STAY.

GONNA MISS YOU SCAPERS ----- YOU WAS NICE QUIET LI'L TADS.

HUMPH!

WHAT'S EATIN' YOU, ALBERT?

I FEELS SICK.

IT'S YO' CONSCIENCE.

DO IT SHOW?

THAT PORKYPINE BEEN GONE TWO WHOLE RAINY DAYS...

BUT HE WERE BOUND HE'D GO!

IF HE'S BOUND TO GO... I IS GONE WALK WITH HIM A WAYS.

THEY'S TWO DAYS TO CATCH UP ON, BUT WAIT FOR COUSIN!

WHY DO IT GOTTA RAIN WHEN US IS LOOKIN' FOR SOME BODY?

IT'S PART OF THE PITY OF IT ALL.

THAT PORKYPINE COULDN'T GIT LOST IN SUNSHINE.

WOULDN'T BE IN CHARACTER

HE MIGHT NOT EVEN BE THE RIGHT PORKYPINE.

WELL, PERSON'LY...

ANY LOST CRITTUR WE FINDS IN THIS STORM WILL BE RIGHT ENOUGH FOR ME.

— 87 —

London Calling:
Kelly Interviewed by the *Sunday Times*

In fall 1959, Walt Kelly was interviewed by Henry Brandon, Washington correspondent for the Sunday Times *of London. Brandon offered the transcript of the interview to Kelly for his perusal. It is published as Kelly edited it — an interview few Americans have ever read.*

AN INTERVIEW WITH WALT KELLY

BRANDON: I think there are today 40 million — or is it more — American readers who read comic strips.

KELLY: It's according to which man you talk to. Whether you speak to the syndicate proprietor or to the national comic strip artist. We have about 55 million circulation in newspapers in this country, and we sort of assume that anybody reading a newspaper reads a comic strip. Now, this is not quite true: *The Wall Street Journal*, for one, does not carry comics; *The New York Times* does not carry comics; and there are others.

BRANDON: What do you think is the reason for the popularity of the comics here?

KELLY: It's probably the same sort of desire for relief or escape — and I prefer the word "relief" — that most people have everywhere. Some people chew — what do they call them? — betel nuts; and other people take opium, and so on; and here we take comic strips.

BRANDON: Well, some people read books.

KELLY: Some people read books and some people look at television and I regret that they look at television, but on the other hand it's not too dissimilar from our business. I think the picture story has always been an engrossing sort of way of delivering a message; it captures the attention of almost anybody.

BRANDON: But in Europe, for instance, you find that there are very few newspapers that carry comic strips. It is, really, primarily an American phenomenon.

KELLY: Yes, and I'm not sure why that is. Of course, if you go back into the origins of comic strips you'll find that they started along about the early part of the nineties as a result of various attempts on the part of newspaper proprietors here to increase their circulation. And comic strips, as a matter of fact, in this country are almost really the result of an accident in trying to put color into a fast-moving press, one of our original rotary-types of press. This accident resulted in Sunday pages. It wasn't until about 1905, I think, that we tried daily strips. The daily strip then, for some reason, got even more popular than the Sunday one. At that time the strips were not syndicated on a national basis. But after a while the people who sell features, and, in fact, the publishers of the large newspapers themselves, formed what we here call "syndicates." For example, if an artist were to make a hundred pounds a week, he would make one pound from each of a hundred papers — rather than make a hundred pounds out of one newspaper. The syndicate term began to be used as a generic term for a man who distributed comic strips.

Now *why* we like comics, I don't know. Our taste earlier ran to such things as what we call "dime novels," the penny thriller, that sort of thing. And we did a great business in that all through the last half of the last century and the early part of this one. You experienced that sort of phenomenon over in your own country.

But *why* we like comics, I'm not quite sure. It might be, it's a possibility, that their popularity is quite over-rated. I don't think anyone has ever quite tested that.

BRANDON: Weren't they originally for children?

KELLY: They originally were, yes.

BRANDON: Then you could — I mean, in an overly facile way — come to the conclusion that Americans are very childish.

KELLY: I wouldn't be the one to leap at that immediately, but I think there is a good deal in that. I think that this is a part of the growing-up of this country. Well, I heard the other day about a man who was going to psychoanalyze a whole Mexican village, and he's not going to psychoanalyze the people in it, he's going to psychoanalyze the village. And I think if you were to psychoanalyze the United States, you would find it still in the growing pains of an adolescent country. I think that a lot of the things that we went through since the last war are indications of how youthful we are — not youthful so much as young — abominably young many times, too many times. Our trouble with [U.S. Senator Joseph] McCarthy, our fear of spies. . .they had stopped in Keystone comedy policemen and villains and they were, in fact, under every bed. We are a young people and this is part of the reason that we look at comics. I do think you might be quite right. We are somewhat amused by childish things: we like to draw mustaches on posters in the subway and so on. And you won't find just children doing this, you'll find rather elderly old ladies doing this sort of thing. (LAUGHS)

I think, actually, that our obsession with motion pictures, our desire to have not a good car but a new car — all these things are manifestations of our continued growing process. And, of course, if we don't grow a little faster, why, the Russians will have grown before we! (LAUGHS) They'll own the moon and we won't have a thing; have nothing but ourselves. What a pity.

I guess comic strips are an indication—here in this country, at least—we are still delighted and obsessed with a picture story. In my own comic strip I have tried to go a little differently and present not so much picture as word. I try to give them some thought. There are probably not more than three or four men in the country who care that much about their work. I don't say that we care more; I think that we're just a little more self-conscious than some and not quite as willing to take the money and not worry about what we're doing for it. We might even feel a little guilty about getting paid so much money for doing so little. Why, some of us spend time working on what we have to say. And, of course, if you spend time working on something to say, you'll eventually find something to say.

BRANDON: Was your comic strip the first serious comic strip?

KELLY: I don't think it's entirely the first. I think Al Capp has always tried to put some sort of satirical—if not philosophical comment—but certainly satirical...and very often political parody gets into his work. And he's done that now for 25 years. When that [aspect] first moved into it, I don't know. There was a comic strip called Krazy Kat which ran many years ago. The man who drew it, George Herriman, died about 1944. He had drawn it since 1915, or 1920—I'm not sure—it may even have been before that, but it was in that period. And whereas he did not actually come out with philosophical statements, still he had an underlying philosophy behind it which was that the gentle will survive. He was serious to that extent. Capp, on the other hand, is serious to the extent of wishing to make fun and poke holes in people who are a little too pompous. My strip does somewhat the same thing. Mine is a more continuous allegorical expression, actually, than any of the others, which doesn't particularly make it a good comic strip, but it certainly does what I want it to do.

BRANDON: What is your basic philosophy?

KELLY: Oh, I think that life goes on in spite of everything we do. We can't keep it from going on. (LAUGHS) We manage to survive despite ourselves. No matter what we do to enhance our position or to make it worse, why, we remain just about where the good Lord intended us to be at the moment.

BRANDON: Well, don't you then encourage the idea that there isn't really very much we can do about ourselves—

KELLY: I'm not sure that I don't...I think you're right. I think this might be my philosophy. And this is not a philosophy of weariness so much as it is one of knowing that we are what we are, and we can always try to be better. But very little we do will actually change the kind of people we are. We can always expect the "boob," as we call the fool in America, to show up. There were a number of little children waiting for a school bus to come along the other day...some damn ex-convict had stolen an automobile and he charged into thirty of them—killed three or four. This sort of accident comes up constantly—the fool or the boob—upsetting all the best-laid plans of mice and men—a continuing discouraging manifestation. Not that I'm weary, not that I think people should be weary, but I don't think we should be too upset if something comes along to upset an apple-cart, or our children. We can expect a lot of this.

BRANDON: But you said earlier the American people, you think, are very youthful and in the process of maturing.

KELLY: I would hope they're in the process of maturing. I'm not sure they are always, and I don't think anyone else is. But we do seem to be gaining some sense as we go along. We do show signs of improving. Oh, for example, we probably would not go in again—right away, at least—for the McCarthy period. We probably would not. I don't know now whether we would drop the atomic bomb; I think there might be a little sentiment against that sort of thing.

BRANDON: But, you don't think it is part of your aim in your comic strip to bring this home and to help this process of maturing?

KELLY: Well, yes, I think it is. It is not only my aim; I think it is my obligation not only to remind us how youthful and how brainless we are, but also within the same framework to hold out hope for the future. I don't mean there's no possibility of any hope. I merely like to state over and over again that we shouldn't ever expect too much of ourselves because we're very frail and we're inclined to break very easily. And I think my philosophy is not unlike that of the Reverend Dodgson—Lewis Carrol. We can expect the falls and the bolts, and we can expect ourselves to be very frail, and I think their presence (?) sometimes is very frightening. I think his trial scene—the Knave who sole the tarts—[is] one of the greatest pieces of satirical writing. Whether he intended it that way or not, I don't know, but it certainly fit our whole McCarthy period. The poem that the

White Rabbit found and read: "They told me that you had been to her," and so on. A great piece of work — absolutely meaningless and yet accepted with the gratest respect by the court. And this is exactly what we did! We did this for about the last ten or fifteen years.... We only stopped doing it about four years. And the reason largely was because McCarthy, in our country, finally got in trouble with his own private court, the Senate. It wasn't that he had caused others to suspect well-meaning citizens; it was that McCarthy had overstepped particular house rules in the Senate; he had been a whore to his fellow members. And this annoyed the Senate so much that they finally took him down. His crime was not against the American people; it was against the Club, and that's exactly why he went down; he didn't go down for any other reason.

This, I think, is great comedy material. So, I parodied that in my own way in the strip. I try to find out what we would call "screwball" or "offbeat" here — what is incongruous in our makeup. Mr. Khrushchev's visit here was hilarious and I treated it in the strip that way. All these people, the big candidates rushing over to see Mr. Khrushchev — just as they did in your country. Candidates do this, you see — they're pretty busy checking in with the bear. They must go over and check with Khruschchev before they can run. We've been doing that. Nixon went over, Eisenhower will be going over pretty soon, we had Hubert Humphrey over there, and we had a few others. And you, of course, had Mr. Macmillan and the labor leaders. I think this is all pretty funny stuff. In order to run for office in your own country you must check in with Russia! I don't see anything in it but that all these people think this will bring them Page One attention in the newspapers; this is the big reason they do it. I'm sure that Mr. Eisenhower doesn't have that in mind, but I'm sure Mr. Nixon welcomed that trip to Russia. And I would expect that sometime in the future we might see Mr. Rockefeller go over there. And if we can find a real, sure-enough, Democratic party candidate, he may take a trip to Russia. Mr. Stevenson has already been there.

BRANDON: Well, you really have your finger on the pulse of this country perhaps better than most. I mean, you feel the weaknesses and the strengths of this country. We've talked mainly of the weaknesses. What do you think are the strengths?

KELLY: I think the strength is...I think it was quite manifest when Mr. Khrushchev came here, that without any instruction from anyone in particular our people just turned out and looked at him as if he were a curiosity. They stood back and, in fact, did not treat him with discourtesy so much as they treated him with apathy. They were not really impressed by him; they were not really impressed by this whole visit, but they were curious. I think therein lies two of our strengths. First of all, we are curious and we will continue to probe for those things that we think we want. We will search for them. Secondly, we are not too impressed with other people's strength at this moment. We are certainly, and almost with alarm, finding ourselves in a position of strength, of real strength, of world leadership. And I think we are taking it rather well, on the whole, not too bad, not [being] too pompous about it. I think there's a quiet feeling about the strength rather than a feeling of being able to intimidate anybody or threaten anyone. I think we're amazed at finding ourselves in this position because we had felt that you people had that position for so long and that within my lifetime — 45 years — this position has changed. And, I might say, much to our

regret! We would rather be where we were — having you out front. But now we find we're there — we're taken aback — and yet we feel quiet about it. We really don't want us to have any trouble. And at the same time — I think we showed this at Khrushchev's visit — we don't intend to have anybody push us around, despite whatever weapons they have. Whether we intend to let anybody else push other people around, I don't know; I'm not sure of that.

BRANDON: Do you think Americans are basically people with a sense of humor?

KELLY: I think they are, generally. I think that any group of people who are on the way up have room within their minds to laugh at themselves. For all too damn long we laughed at other people, and now we are beginning to find ourselves rather funny. I think the British developed that style of humor, of self-expression, to a high degree — and it's still going on. I think we're just beginning to get at that...what we call the pratfall doesn't work quite so well as it did at one time. We can work in innuendo now, and suggestions, and with more subtle grace than at one time. We don't have to hit a man on the head in order to get a laugh.

And so I think we still have room — and your people still have room — to laugh at themselves. We may not see any sign of it, but I suppose the Russians have room to laugh at themselves. I think, however, that they are more inclined to take themselves rather seriously. The thing that I've always liked about the Chinese, for example, is that they can always laugh at themselves, even in the worst situation. The Indians, on the other hand, I don't think have a very great sense of humor. And I think that these things *do* run racially. I hesitate to be racial about anything, but numbers of us are inclined to take ourselves seriously and others are inclined to find room for

laughter. I don't think we have any bitter laughter in us because we haven't lost that much yet, whereas the Mediterranean people have quite a bit of bitter laughter; they've lost so much so often.

BRANDON: Therefore, what kind of humor do you think has the main appeal here? Slapstick humor or —

KELLY: Well, the exaggerated, incongruous form of humor. One of the forms has been what we call the "shaggy dog" story, a greatly exaggerated story usually involving an animal. [There's] the story about the man who came in [to a bar] with the mouse and the frog. The mouse stood up and sang and the frog played the piano. The bartender said, "How can that mouse sing like that?" And the fellow said, "Because the frog is a ventriloquist." You see, this sort of thing. It doesn't really mean anything. There's actually no point to the story, but it goes from one exaggeration to another and the second exaggeration is supposedly an explanation of the first. I think we like that sort of thing pretty well — not that that's our only diet.

BRANDON: Is this the reason you chose animals for your strip?

KELLY: No, I chose animals largely because you can do more with animals. They don't hurt as easily, and its possible to make them more believable in an exaggerated pose, than it is the human. The characters in the strip are all representations of me, I guess — all of them — rather than Pogo. I would guess that as the cartoonist, as the artist, as the commentator, you might consider me as Pogo, sure. But the other people are also me and, unfortunately, my friends find this all too true at times. As I say, we actually have no heroes as such in the strip because I don't believe in heroes. We have no good, we

have no evil, because I don't believe in either. My villains eventually get to be almost like other people and it's a real effort to keep them from becoming rather tiresome.

BRANDON: How far in advance do you prepare your strips?

KELLY: Well, the syndicates and the newspapers always like to stay about eight weeks in advance, but because I like to stay as topical as I can and because I'm sure something will always come up that I'd like to comment on, I try to keep it somewhere between four and six weeks. Even then it gets rather difficult to forecast what is going to happen six weeks, four weeks, ahead of time. For example, I have a sequence coming on this moonshot that the Russians made. I was able to file it just by a month, but I wish I had known about it a little in advance because I could have hit it right on the nose. I put up the theory that the Russian moonshot—that round ball of

instruments that they declare landed on September 13 at 5:22 or something—actually landed in a swamp in Okefenokee, and we have it down there now, and they've just opened it up and found two seals waving Russian pennants. These seals are convinced that they're on the moon and they want to be taken to the cheese mines and to find out the secrets of the moon. They're a little disturbed to find that the Americans are on the moon and have beaten them to it. They're a bit afraid to go back to tell Nikita this, so they may stay in the swamp, you see ...that sort of thing. I would like to have hit that right on the nose, but not knowing, I couldn't. But we did have some idea when Mr. Khrushchev would arrive here, so I was able to pick September 15th, when he did arrive in the strip as a bear, all dressed up as an old-time American capitalist with a dollar-spangled vest, a frock coat, a silk hat, a gold-headed cane, a watch chain and all that sort of thing. When he landed he said, "Take me to your President."

THE MILWAUKEE JOURNAL

INSIGHT

Sunday FEBRUARY 22, 1970

In Pogo's swampland, Washington's birthday is a crashing success

Drawn exclusively for INSIGHT
by Walt Kelly

Wisconsin

INSIGHT

SUNDAY MAGAZINE OF THE MILWAUKEE JOURNAL

February 22, 1970

EDITOR
George J. Lockwood

ASSISTANT EDITOR
Donald E. Magarian

FROM THE EDITOR

It is comforting in this unsettled time to have an alter ego, some Jiminy Cricket whispering into our ear that *all is not well*. Cartoonist Walt Kelly is just such a man, and *Insight* is proud to publish both an original cover drawing and an article. . .by this very humorous and profound human being. For twenty years now, Walt Kelly, through the creatures in his famed comic strip Pogo, has been telling us all is not well. He warned us during the Joe McCarthy era that political excesses were dangerous to our democracy. In the 1950s, after the Supreme Court overruled segregation, he pointedly discussed the obligations of educating black children in white schools. Tonight at 7:30 over channel 4, Kelly will try to illuminate a pressing contemporary problem: the need for understanding in an age of violent disagreement.

But let Walt Kelly tell it: "Humor, bathos and pathos can all spring from the same source. Often it is misconception or complete noncomprehension. Motion pictures, like comic strips, borrow from life to bring about incongruous situations. In the 'Pogo Special,' the running motivation is misunderstanding. Miss Ma'm'selle Hepzibah misunderstands Pogo's eloquence on behalf of a friend. Albert and Beauregard misunderstand each other's conception of a Christmas carol. Churchy LaFemme and Howland Owl (lower left) misunderstand the needs of youth and hawk firecrackers. Miz Bug (lower right) misunderstands her son Fremont's need of reassurance and buys him a cannon cracker. And, finally, Porkypine misunderstands all the activity and thinks he's being left out of a party."

– GEORGE J. LOCKWOOD

THE QUIZZICAL KIDS:

An understanding cartoonist appraises the youth of today and finds them NOT wanting

By Walt Kelly

Once upon a long time ago when the terminative dinosaur had groaned his last, a band of apparently well-behaved children, well-informed to a point, bright as glaciers in the sun, and obviously contained, held forth on radio.

We, their somewhat elders, were amazed, pleased

and made comfy by their act which consisted of answering world-shaking questions, to wit: How many feet to a rooster? (Answer: According to how tall he is.) And why is a blackberry red when it's green? (Don't remember the answer.)

The amazement came at the thought that the young could appear smarter than we were; we were pleased (vicariously, to be sure) that the kids made a nice piece of change out of these Sunday shenanigans; and we were comfy because all this was a very safe smartness. Theirs was a contained, sterilized brilliance. We, the elders, were not likely to be shown up. The children were known as the Quiz Kids.

Now, in this year of 1970, a good many of us have progressed to a plateau where we no longer need to borrow a lawnmower for that fast Saturday trip around the yard. The family rug no longer doubles as an overcoat. We are affluent to the point of letting our bills lag; some of us have two and a half cars; and quite a few insist on buying drinks for strangers. Too many of our set have become dedicated to the resolute mugwumpery of *stare decisis* which approximately means being independent of any movement, forward, backward or sideways.

In the comfort of our fortified hummock in this swamp of our own making we have lately been hearing strange grunts and pipings from the surrounding pads. These are noises of a new bunch of kids, somewhat more quizzical than the aforementioned.

This crowd is not answering questions. They are asking. And the questions asked are rather rude, even jolting. We have been quick to admit that these kids are indeed quizzical — that is to say, sort of odd, a bit eccentric, on the weird side.

Also, we freely grant that they are quizzical in the sense of being bantering, teasing, even annoying. If we listen to the winds stirring the night grasses we may learn they also are quizzical in the present sense of being inquiring, inquisitive and, most disrespectfully, not always believing the first answer to anything.

Ipso facto, keeping a sharp eye on the pads around the hummock, we conclude that theirs is not a contained brilliance. It makes a man worry. His security is insecure.

And yet, was security ever secure? Was safety ever safe? Remember Santa Claus? Poof, revelation! And the psychological peace of mind of a seven-year-old is blasted. You hold on, though, to the shred that at least there was a St. Nicholas, and then the church throws him out of the lodge. Ashes. After you lose Santa Claus somebody comes along and tells you that Parson Weems invented the whole thing about the cherry tree and George Washington. You begin to wonder if George Washington ever did tell a lie. Could a boy who would chop down a cherry tree lead his countrymen in a fight for freedom and find happiness in being the Father of His Country? Muddled, you reason that he didn't do it when he was a boy anyway.

So, innocence is gradually cast adrift. Other beliefs go until the adult human, believing in his own maturity, figures that his remaining innocence, his true spirit and his safety should be protected by solid walls. We forget about China and we dismiss the wall in Berlin as having no meaning for us.

We laugh at but do not really believe Mark Twain. He pointed out that when he was quite young he thought his father was the greatest mental lout east of the Pacific. When he was older, in his twenties, he was surprised at how much the old boy had learned in a few years. Mr. Clemens, the younger, gladly demonstrates here that we are all pretty much alike. We agree, generally, but did we ever feel that way about our fathers? We're convinced that our kids feel that way about us at times, despite surveys by reputable social scientists showing that they, most of them, do not.

Like the elder Mr. Clemens, we all contain a modicum of flaw and imperfection. If a man lacks a mother-in-law with the eye of a chicken hawk, it does no harm to have the children substitute as critics. Criticism is not always sheerly antagonistic. And, as the old age of twenty-one creaks their joints and levels their minds, the children may change. So may we.

Certainly, insularity does not protect us from others in the world. There can be no wall between us and our neighbor. Strictly speaking, our children are our neighbors. Therefore, no wall between us and our children.

The biggest reason for this is that we are all children. An outstanding example in proof of this theory is a cursory look at any clutch of our national, state or provincial political leaders. They are great sources of humorous action, childlike at times, and we, looking to them as leaders, demonstrate our own childishness.

We expect the big boys in the sandbox to have more on the ball than we, whereas they merely have bigger pails, more shovels and not all of these their own. Maybe we thought our parents should have more on the ball, too. When these expectations have failed of fruition over the years, we, the "beleagured and exhausted," have learned to shrug and grin. French historians have pointed out that such "maturity" resulted in the fall of France. Our children, so far, are not learning the shift of going along. They are not shrugging. They are asking very unpleasant questions. Loudly.

True, the kids ask the questions in a jargon we elders dimly understand. Many of them dress in weird fashion, a cross between a far-out gypsy and a second-rate burlesque comedian. In other words, they refuse to conform to the strictures of a society they are not endorsing. And in this they, of course, are setting up their own wall and, in conforming to themselves, they are establishing their own stereotype. But at least they are not contained in a box not of their own making.

We, too, all those centuries ago, spoke in strange tongues and dressed strangely. The twenties, the thirties, the forties were all part of the same revolution, if a liberal evolution can be called such. Is it for us, the elderly, to attempt to stay the burgeoning of modern youth, a fifty-year-old movement that has brought us the fruits we now enjoy and/or deplore? We could, rather, spend our time listening and trying to understand, not only the kids, but ourselves.

The personal hummock in our common swamp is frail. The tough mind is very often an attempt to retain the property of self. If we identify with possessions and powers that are transient, how is it possible to scoff at the youth, who, for at least this one young blinding moment, realizes that these are not the things he yearns for? Putting ourselves in his place, is it not possible that we, too, would ask, "Who am I?"

We old grumps will remember that one of the drives of our youth was to "make the world safe for democracy." Now, as goblins loom on every side, we are with George Washington. We cannot tell a lie. Youth looks at the big bomb, big government, big labor, big crime, big britches, and we must admit with him, in the words of a Pogo character, "We gotta make democracy safe for the world."

Green-eared, drag pants, guitar-ridden youth, alert and aware, thinks we're too big for our britches. I agree. The quizzical kids need answers. They'll handle the questions.

*Misunderstanding, sad Porkypine
thinks he's being left out of a party.*

WANTED!

Several million *alert, skillful, personable, able,* young persons (like above) for jobs that pay money in America's factories, businesses, and farms . . .

Secretary of Labor James P. Mitchell says: "Your high school diploma is your passport to a good and useful life. Make the most of your abilities -- prepare for a good job. Finish your schooling. Get your diploma!"

STAY IN SCHOOL & GRADUATE!

It's Not All Rock & Roll In That Tree-Top, Baby

TO AVOID THIS

Do Any One of the Following Things:

1. Finish School and Get Your Diploma.
2. Finish School and Get Your Diploma.
3. Finish School and Get Your Diploma.
4. Marry a Wealthy Person of the Opposite Sex.
5. *GET BACK TO SCHOOL AND GET THAT DIPLOMA!*

NATIONAL BACK-TO-SCHOOL COMMITTEE
Washington 25, D. C.

POGO'S EARLY NOTICES IN THE PRESS

> This section traces the possum's progress, _first in the trade press_, then in Editor & Publisher _magazine articles of December 11, 1948 and December 18, 1948, and then in the general national media with a_ Newsweek _article on Pogo and Walt Kelly that the syndicate used as an effective sales tool. Kelly was always available and ready to accommodate the press. Note the special drawing done for one of the_ Editor & Publisher _articles._

Washington Star, 1950
"Just between Ourselves"
by Philip Love

In last Sunday's "Letters to The Star" column, Reader Eva Meyerson tagged the daily "Pogo" comic strip as "wonderful" and added: "We have not yet been able to identify the dialect, but we find ourselves greeting it with exuberant delight. 'Caterpiggles,' particularly, are wonderful."

Well, the dialect is "pure Florida-Georgia cracker." I'm assured by Robert M. Hall, president of the Post-Hall Syndicate, Inc., which distributes "Pogo."

The swamp in which Pogo Possum and his pals cavort is the Okefenokee, in Georgia. That's why they called their Christmas carolers the "Okefenokee Glee and Pilau Society." Pilau, to save you the trouble of looking it up in a dictionary, is a dish made of rice or cracked wheat boiled with meat, fish or fowl and spices.

Cartoonist Walt Kelly created Pogo, Howland Owl, Porkypine, Rackety Coon and the other swamplings for a comic book, then made them into a daily strip for the New York _Star_. When that newspaper suspended publication, he was deluged with letters demanding that the comic be continued in some other paper. He took the letters and samples of the strip to Mr. Hall, who became convinced that Pogo was one 'possum with a future.

• • •

Pogo no sooner began appearing in this newspaper than letters of commendation began coming in from readers. "Wonderful," "delightful" and "delicious" were among the adjectives used. Now hardly a day passes that someone doesn't write or phone to exclaim over

Pogo. Reader Meyerson's note was but one of four received that same week, and there were three phone calls, besides.

While the Okefenokee Glee and Pilau Society was doing its caroling, a man phoned to chortle: "That Pogo! Ha-ha! 'Deck me out in Boston Charlie,' whatever that is! It's wonderful! Ha-ha!"

For such an enthusiastic customer, I should have said something clever, I suppose. But the best I could manage was a bit of assistance on the last ha-ha. That must have satisfied him, however, because he hung up.

So far, only two people have told me they don't like Pogo. Both, I regret to say, are members of the *Star* staff. One buttonholed me to demand: "Say, what dimwit around here is responsible for our having that awful comic, Pogo?"

"I guess I am," I confessed.

"We-w-well," he stammered, "maybe it's better than it looks. I—I haven't really read it. Just looked at it, y'know. Something like Donald Duck, isn't it?"

"No, it isn't the least bit like Donald Duck or any other comic. You ought to read it."

"Yes," he conceded, still somewhat red-faced, "I guess I ought to."

The other anti came to the door of my office carrying that day's *Star*, opened to the comics pages. "This Pogo," he said, holding out the paper, "is no good to begin with, and today it's the all-time low in comics. Read it."

Midway through it, I started to laugh. Strangely enough, he laughed, too. Then a nasty suspicion entered his mind. "You're — ha-ha — ribbing me," he charged. "No, I'm not," I insisted. "To me, it's — ha-ha — very funny." We both laughed some more.

Another member of the staff strolled by. "Bet I know what you're laughing at," she ventured. "Pogo! Isn't it simply hilarious?"

Well, anyway, fellow members of the Okefenokee Glee and Pilau Society, Pogo and his pals will appear in the *Star* on Sundays, too, starting three weeks from today — January 29, that is.

KELLY LOOKS, ACTS
LIKE HIS ANIMALS

Walt Kelly is a plumpish man of 38 with a catlike mustache and owl-like tortoise-shell glasses, who once worked as a cartoonist for Walt Disney. He conceived his swampland characterizations in 1942 for comic books, later put them in a newspaper strip which was syndicated only three years ago. In *Pogo*, Kelly maintains that he is mostly satirizing himself. As shown in his drawings below, he gurgles, grunts and grimaces with them, his own reactions to situations becoming their reactions, and vice versa. His method of working is simply to drop Pogo and Albert into a situation and then try to figure out how he might react under the circumstances. His method, he explains, is like that of the old Keystone cops of the movies who used to get together for a day's shooting and say, "Let's go into a barbershop and see what happens."

OVERLY SERIOUS, Kelly scowls like Howland Owl. The owl is a pseudo scientist who thinks he knows everything but constantly makes a mess of things.

GAY AND FEY like Albert the Alligator, Kelly smokes his cigar. Albert is a know-it-all but unlike Owl he can, when pressed, rise to occasion and be a hero.

PUFFED UP, Kelly jauntily swings along with Beauregard Bugleboy the dog. Beauregard has never been able to get over the fact he is man's best friend.

Pogo's Progress

Ever since Aesop, smart satirists have used stories of animals to reflect the follies and foibles of human beings. Ever since George Herriman's sparkling "Krazy Kat," comic-strippers have tried the same thing. Last week there began the newspaper syndication of a cartoon cast made up of perhaps the most satirically lifelike wildlife since "Uncle Remus." Its star: a pug-nosed, pensive little possum named Pogo.

Wide-eyed and fuzzy, the half-pint Pogo could well be the sometimes oppressed and almost always bewildered average guy. Often he is the pawn for his Southern swampland cronies. They are the slickly suave Albert Alligator, the intellectual Howlan' Owl, a carefree turtle called Churchy La Femme, and sourpuss Porkypine. There is Mis' Hop Frog, who dupes Pogo into tadsitting, and a mailman duck whose webbed feet

ache. All drawl a sort of cracker talk. When Pogo and his pals first appeared in the funnies—in the short-lived New York Star—their animal antics delighted children. But mainly it was adults who liked the strip's sharp, high comedy. College professors wrote fan letters.

Pogo is the strip-child of Walt Kelly, 35, a big and bespectacled ex-reporter and onetime Disney animator. Kelly, like Albert Alligator, is almost a chain cigar smoker. He draws in a "tired" old Connecticut house in Darien, beside a swamp in which, says the cartoonist, roam some of New England's not too numerous opossums.

While still in high school, Kelly became a news hound and then a cartoonist for The Bridgeport Post and Telegram. He first began to sketch Pogo in 1942 in comics books. At that time Pogo simply was a spear bearer in another story, but fan mail (rare in comics-book making) built the little possum into stardom.

When Kelly went to The Star last year as a political cartoonist (he was famous for his Mechanical Man drawings of Governor Dewey), he took Pogo along. It was the Post Hall Syndicate, a New York Post Home News subsidiary, that last week began to syndicate him to other papers.

Urged this week by grumpy Porkypine to hang like a possum from a tree limb—by his tail—Pogo significantly replied: "I is more the human bean type."

Kelly (by Kelly), Pogo, and friends

Walt Kelly's 'Pogo' Ribs Stupidities of Mankind

By DORIS WILLENS

Walt Kelly would like some day to be known as the A. A. Milne of comic stripdom.

The warmth and humanity of the Britisher's child books are what Kelly is striving for in his strip, "Pogo," which has made its appearance in the New York *Star*.

"I sometimes think we've lost something of the human element in becoming so slick and modern in our living, in our writing," explained Kelly in a voice that hasn't a trace of the complex Southern dialects his animal characters use in "Pogo."

Like most cartoonists whose main characters are animals, Kelly uses "Pogo," an opossum, alligators, owls, turkeys, etc., to portray human beings.

Kelly's animals inhabit the swamplands of the South.

"I've always been fascinated by the swamplands. And they're one of the last frontiers for comic strips. So I chose them for my background," related Kelly, who has been drawing "Pogo" comic books for five years, poking gentle fun at the frailties and stupidities of man.

"What I'm trying to show is that we're all at fault," he said. "We all do many of the stupid, unthinking things my animals do. And I'm also trying to illustrate that old cliche – that under many a hard exterior beats a heart of gold."

HORNS OF DILEMMA

In attempting to capture the "charming British warmth" of the best in children's books, Kelly finds himself running into the same dilemma as Milne and Lewis Carroll. The adults, rather than the children, are its staunchest supporters.

"You have to grow up to a book like Alice in Wonderland," according to Kelly.

And from the fan mail Kelly has received since "Pogo" began his career some five years ago, it is obvious the strip is for adults. Kelly has stacks of mail from college students and college professors; very little from the youngsters.

"My six-year-old daughter won't even read it," he said, "She'd much rather read fairy tales."

Kelly started the strip using the standard (or what is thought by Northerners to be standard) Southern dialect. He was accused of poking fun at Negroes and poor Whites. So he switched to straight English.

But after experimenting, he turned to a dialect that combines the Elizabethan English still found in the South, the French of New Orleans, the Negro and the Indian.

STUDENT OF DIALECT

Kelly has studied phonetics, dialects, anthropology as well as social problems of the South.

Raised in Connecticut, he was an animator for Walt Disney for six years on the West Coast, has illustrated educational pamphlets for the Army, still does comic books, commercial cartoons and illustrations for children's books.

He was hired by the *Star* as political cartoonist, and has expanded his work with the paper to include "Pogo," weather cartoons and supervision of all art work.

His "mechanical man" cartoons of Governor Dewey were among the most devastating of anti-Dewey drawings. Kelly put Dewey into an adding machine, a cash register, a tank, a music box, the body of a robot, and just about every other mechanical device he could think of.

'EASIER TO TEAR DOWN'

"When you're in favor of a person, you use superlatives and make them damned dull people," he said. "I had plenty of complaints because I wasn't running enough pro-Truman cartoons. But I couldn't sink my teeth into him. I figured the best thing I could do was tear down his opponent.

"When you are FOR an individual, you stand a good chance of becoming mealy-mouthed. Positive ends are hard to put into symbols."

Kelly follows the sentiments of "Pogo" – that only he without sin should cast a stone – in his political cartooning.

"It's tough to throw a stone at a man like, say, Mayor O'Dwyer. If he does something I dislike today, I hate to criticize him because I might make the same mistake tomorrow.

"But some men become representative of a philosophy of life that is so evil that they become symbols – you can throw a stone at those people."

Which is why he does "Pogo."

"If you can fight the stupidities themselves, rather than a particular stupid act, without annoying your readers, then you've really got something," Kelly said.

"Pogo" Artist Walt Kelly, and friends from swamplands, drawn specially for E&P.

N.Y. Star Features Become Star Syndicate

By Ogden J. Rochelle

THE NEW YORK STAR SYNDICATE, which grew from out-of-town demand for *New York Star* features, up to now an over-the-transom business, will take to the road, Jan. 3, with a full sales kit.

Most of the comics and features to be offered are done by Star staffers, but Fred Methot, syndicate manager, has added some new ones. Methot, formerly with UNITED FEATURE SYNDICATE, says he will try to offer editors a "complete promotion service" for use with every feature.

Methot

Leading off the syndicate's roster of artists is Bill Mauldin, Pulitzer prize cartoonist of World War II fame.

Mauldin on 'New Army'

Mauldin is being sent to Camp Bliss or Camp Hood at the first of the year to work out a series on the "New Army." The series, at the rate of four panels a week, is expected to be ready by Jan. 18.

Mauldin, now 27, was first handled by UFS. He served in the Army, and found the period of re-adjustment a difficult one that took a long vacation and a second best-seller. The first book was "Up Front," to solve. "Back Home," to solve.

While in high school at Phoenix, Ariz., Mauldin took a correspondence course in cartooning and later studied at the Academy of Fine Arts in Chicago, working his way.

On returning to Phoenix he drew cartoons for both sides of a local political campaign and joined the Arizona National Guard. Shortly after came the war. The rest of Mauldin's story has been told in his books and the "Willie and Joe" cartoons.

This fall, Mauldin returned to cartooning with a series on city kids for the New York Star, a feature less acrid but not less searching than his former series.

Other Star Items

Little Pedro by William de la Terre, a pantomime of Mexican characters, which has been in the *New Yorker* magazine for four years, will receive its first newspaper promotion in Star Syndicate's sales kit. Sample sequences will go out in an original general mailing of 500, intensively aimed at the Southwest.

"Pogo," an animals strip that grown-ups go for more than the youngsters, is by Walt Kelly, the Star's art director, who for the Star also does political cartoons and weather vanes. (E&P, Dec. 11, p. 42.)

One of Walt Kelly's pre-election panels, envisioning Dewey and Truman in a poker game, is one of two cartoons out of the welter in the last campaign that the President elected to hang in the White House. (It was reprinted in E&P, Nov. 6, p. 6.) The other cartoon is by Mauldin.

Also in Methot's bag of tricks will be the strip, Barnaby, featuring a ghost character, now being drawn by Jack Morley. This feature was formerly a CHICAGO SUN-TIMES SYNDICATE release.

Carries Columnist Deutsch

Text releases by the Star will include several columnists, among them Albert Deutsch, twice a winner of the Heywood Broun award.

Anne Shirley's Hollywood gossip column, Tom Meany on sports, and Gerald W. Johnson on politics and government, will be Star syndicate leaders.

Also for daily release will be Jennings Perry, columnist, who on Oct. 26 came close to predicting an election. "It's Closer Than You Think," said his headline.

A once-a-week release will be Irma Simonton Black's page, "Life With Junior." It's written as a help to parents, and illustrated with panels that appeal to children, by John Pierotti, the Star's sports cartoonist.

Two other weekly columns are by John Lardner and Frank Columbine. Columbine does a column on columnists, a sly review of the inconsistencies and coincidences. Lardner writes a theater review, which is accompanied by a Battaglia illustration.

Feature fillers include a cross-word puzzle and "Let's Play Chess," by Al Horowitz, former U.S. open champion, illustrated with diagramatic chess positions.

Scott Ink Distribution

gives uniform inking at all speeds—Better printing —Does not flood or pale— Less spoilage

Send for Catalog

Walter Scott & Co.
PLAINFIELD, N. J.

Press Alliance Kit Plays Pantomines

IN EUROPE where newspapers do not circulate across a 3,000-mile spread with the native population reading one language, the pantomime comic guage, the pantomime comic reached adulthood long ago.

Among four new strips that Press Alliance will offer to clients in the 1949 season, two are pantomimes, one from Belgium, the other from France.

"Oh, Oswald," from Belgium, by Jean-Leo and Martin, is for sophisticates. Oswald is a romance hunter, but humor is the dominant note.

"Professor Nimbus," by J. Darthel from France plays the absent-minded professor role with variations.

First offering of PA will be "Nanny O'Lace," ready in January, by American artist, Larry Reynolds. Nanny is an intriguing grandmother with adventures, who is pushed into being a detective as effective and tough as the best in who-donits.

Eric Johnston Serialized

Eric Johnston, currently president of the Motion Picture Association, ex-president of the U.S. Chamber of Commerce, one of the most articulate capitalists in the world, is presented by PA for a six-installment series, beginning Jan. 1. The series is excerpted from Johnston's new book, "We're All In It."

Map-Making AP

KUDOES come from Korea for Associated Press background maps by the Newsfeatures service. Recently AP released a background map of Korea, showing transport facilities and the distribution of industries. So accurately was it done by AP's artists and researchers that Korea's government admitted it was better than its own.

"The Korean Government mission here," reads an official letter to the AP bureau in Washington, "says the map is the best of its kind they have seen. They are using it for official reference."

The mission asked for mats and prints of the map.

In existence since 1939, AP background maps has now made its 365th. (E&P, Apr. 10, p. 50).

For the past two months the department has been under David Stein, who replaces Robert Cool, now of the *Providence* (R. I.) *Bulletin*.

AP's map division had a lucky break the other day when the Costa Rica revolution broke. The artists were just finishing a background on South and Central America. A quick change in copy made it available as a spot news feature.

Toodles on Cover

PENNY and Pat, the Toodle Twins of the CHICAGO SUN-TIMES SYNDICATE'S strip, enliven the cover of the fifth annual "Reading for Democracy" book list published by the Chicago Women's division of the National Conference of Christians and Jews. The list shows 68 titles, and the project is part of NCCJ's program to promote "justice, amity, understanding and cooperation among all peoples."

Ripley's Anniversary

ABOUT 100 newspaper and syndicate people costumed in old-fashioned garb for a party in New York's Toots Short's. They celebrated the 30th year of Robert L. Ripley's famed "Believe It or Not," a King Features release.

Cowles Guides FSI

WASHINGTON—Gardner Cowles, president of the *Des Moines* (Ia.) *Register and Tribune*, has been named a member of a 10-man advisory committee of leading Americans, which will guide the Foreign Service Institute in training overseas personnel for the State Department.

EDITOR & PUBLISHER for December 18, 1948

44

Aesop Takes to the Swamp

IN A college classroom, a student drops a comic book practically on the toes of his professor. "I was embarrassed," he writes, "because I didn't want him to think I was a comic book reader. *I am not.* I only read 'Pogo'!" The professor stoops to the floor, picks up the book and remarks: "Hm'mm, a new issue. I must remember to pick one up."

In Chattanooga, Tennessee, a determined four-year-old is nabbed by police some two hundred miles from home. She explains that she has run away from home to see Pogo the Possum.

In a reader's preference poll conducted by a great metropolitian daily, it's "Pogo" by a landslide. Out of 768 replies received during the first two days of the survey, 601 clamor for "Pogo" with the most delighted superlatives the writers can cram into their letters.

"Pogo" is a gravely humorous comic strip whose leading character, Pogo the Possum, is warm-hearted, generous and a little bewildered — the kind of guy we like to imagine ourselves to be. The strip mirrors more than the life of a gang of engaging swampland characters; it is a gently penetrating satire on our human manners and inadequacies, which connoisseurs have compared to George Herriman's "Krazy Kat," or Don Marquis' immortal "archy and mehitabel."

But if the body of archy the cockroach contained the soul of a *vers libre* poet, Pogo Possum's holds that of a perennial optimist — good-humored despite losing encounters with pyromanic ladybugs seeking vengeance on folks who sing "Ladybug, ladybug, fly away home": and with shiftless friends who dupe him into fighting duels defending the honor of the swamp.

The humanity and appeal of the strip was typified recently when Pogo was urged to hang from a tree limb

Churchy La Femme

Albert the Alligator

by his tail. He declined, saying, "I is more the human bean type."

Pogo's cast of supporting characters, denizens who refer to themselves as "nature's screechers," include individuals who prove themselves to be definitely of the "human bean" type. There are Albert the Alligator, a wise-cracking, cigar-chewing rake with a heart of gold; Dr. Howland Owl, a puttering scientific type who once attempted to cross yew trees with geranium plants to produce synthetic yew-ranium; Porkypine, a curt, grumpy misanthrope; and Capt. Churchy La Femme, the turtle, who is an occasionally reformed pirate.

The hosts of lesser creatures include Choo Choo Curtis, the natural-born duck, who acts as the swampland mail carrier. Choo Choo's feet hurt him, but he refuses to become airborne. Porkypine chided him one day and demanded that he take some pride in his work. "I got plenty of pride," was Choo Choo's retort. "And that's the reason I don't fly. You know what pride goeth before, don't you?"

THESE and other carefree swampland citizens, who daily parade their wonderfully wacky antics to the delight of hundreds of thousands of readers, are the creations of a light-hearted, 36-year-old ex-Philadelphian named Walter Crawford Kelly. He describes himself as "an imposingly flabby man," wears heavy-framed glasses and hides behind a neatly pruned mustache and cigar. He could be an insurance actuary or a highly successful bookie.

Despite the deep-South background of the strip,

Howland Owl

Kelly admits that he has never been farther below the Mason-Dixon line than southern California, where he once worked as an animator for another Walt—named Disney.

"The only thing that inspired me toward an involvement with the southern swampland," he says, "was my sincere conviction that people are universally frail. It struck me that perhaps the Southerners as a much-maligned people would not mind being a little more downtrodden." Their good nature and ability to make humorous a rough situation struck Kelly as being a Christian virtue, and it is his hope that "Pogo" will nudge people into a more general awareness that they are all, after all, "human beans."

The dialect spoken by the characters, a mixture of Georgia cracker and pure hokum, liberally salted with malapropisms, comes from Kelly's interest in speech patterns of the Atlantic seaboard. He was fascinated by the mystery of the southern swampland during a research into folkways, and began to think of the Okefenokee region as "a last frontier, a proper setting for American fairy tales."

The characters are not all Georgians, however. Seminole Sam, the wily con man, speaks the cant of the pitchman, while Solid MacHogany, a jazz virtuoso, gives out with pure Bourbon Street patter.

THE IDEA for a comic feature built around the swampland was realized at last in 1942 when Kelly sired a comic book concerning the adventures of a little colored boy named Bumbazine, together with rabbits, turtles, hop-frogs, an alligator and a possum.

The alligator became popular, was named Albert and shared top billing with Bumbazine for awhile. However, Kelly felt that no matter how attractively he might portray the child, there was a chance that some people would be offended. And so Pogo the Possum, who until now had held a strictly subordinate role, assumed Bumbazine's virtues of gentle bewilderment, naivete, friendliness and sturdy common sense, and became the hero of the feature.

After a mild success in the comic book market, Kelly approached the New York *Star* with the idea of a daily Pogo strip. "I was able to persuade them through Bart Crum, an eminent and affable San Francisco attorney of Jesuit upbringing, that the *Star* without Pogo would molder into dust in a matter of weeks." Kelly adds, "Three months after the *Star* accepted 'Pogo,' the newspaper folded."

Nevertheless, such enthusiastic fan mail was received during this initial appearance that several syndicates bid for the new strip, and it was eventually distributed by the New York *Post*. In a little more than two years, "Pogo" has sold to over two hundred papers in the United States and Canada, and bids fair to give such top-notchers as "Blondie," "Li'l Abner" and "Dick Tracy" a run for the big money.

Kelly does his work in an old house in Darien, Connecticut, held together, he says, by paint and inertia. He works at a board in the living room, surrounded by wife Helen, daughters Kathleen and Carolyn, and small son Peter. He has a proper studio which roosts on a rock above the house, but the small Kellys quickly appropriated it and crowded their father out.

KELLY'S good-humored, joshing spirit is all-pervasive in the strip. A gentle spoof on the reading habits of

Porkypine

Americans occurred one time when Pogo and Albert were rowing around the swamp,

"How come this boat is so skimpy like?" complains Albert. Pogo frowns and says, "For us as does the rowin', they can't be made too small. It's all on account of the paper shortage. . . . Ol' publisher says, 'Cut down on them boats; they takes too much room.' Course, from cuttin' down on the boats, next they'll cut down on the size of the critturs. . .till finally, Albert, YOU won't be hardly larger nor a midge fly; and someday us critturs will disappear ENTIRE, and the comic book industry will come to a sad end. . .books with nothin' in but words."

In another incident, do-good pacifists come in for a kidding. Albert has been wrestling with a ferocious diving board and has at last succeeded in getting a half-nelson on it. Two white doves, announcing themselves to be peaceful critturs, come and perch on the tautly bowed board which Albert is holding. They urge him to "cease this struggle – for your own good, desist – turn the bright face of peace upon this. . . ." Albert complies, releasing the board, which promptly flies apart with a loud *sproinggg,* tossing the doves stunningly to the ground. With open mouth, Albert watches from behind a tree as the doves attack the spent board in a rage. When Pogo and Porkypine amble onto the scene and ask what's new, Albert observes: "Oh, nothin'. I was thinkin' it's just natural for a crittur to ack natural."

Pogophiles are among the most enthusiastic and loyal readers in the world. The strip has provoked cries of "Brilliant! – Intellectual! – Utterly enchanting!" from

delighted Ph.D's and bedozzled nine-year-olds alike. But it is plain that the reasons for preference are subtly different.

There are delicious bits in "Pogo" obviously beyond the realm of childish humor, such as the characterization of the pompously officious Deacon Mushrat who speaks in pontifical Gothic typography; or that of P.T. Bridgeport, a wistful bear who is a motheaten circus entrepreneur anxious to make a comeback. His speeches are delivered in the most flamboyantly Barnumese type, garnished with curlicues and accompanied by a stirring snaredrum tattoo.

But universally appealing to both children and grown-ups alike are the antics of swampland young folk like the Rackety-Coon Chile and his Pup-Dog. Kelly's glowing humanism was illustrated typically on the day Pogo and Rackety-Coon set out to find the pot of gold at the end of the rainbow. After many adventures, Rackety-Coon Chile says:

"Uncle Pogo, we started to find the gold at the end of the rainbow, but us didn't get 'round to it. Is they really, truly gold?" Pogo says that he is only a mere possum, but "You had fun lookin' an' that's important. And what you found was a mess of swamplan' friends havin' fun. You got a cozy home to go to, an' a mammy to love you. . . . What mo' you wants, li'l tad?"

"Mushrat say I might of got a gole watch," says Chile, "but then I can't tell time anyway."

And Pogo nods wisely as they go back to join the rest of "nature's screechers," at a moonlit fish-fry in the evening quiet of the swamp.

Pogo

1-10 PUBLISHERS - HALL SYNDICATE INC.

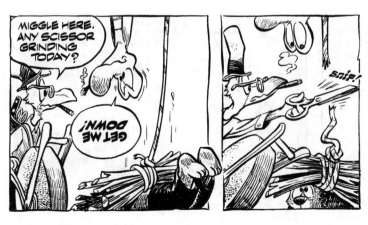

4-4 Publishers-Hall Syndicate Inc.

TADPOLE ALERT

WALT KELLY'S CHRISTMAS CARDS

The tradition of cartoonists creating special Christmas cards dates back to the turn of the century. It's still going strong. Dik ("Hagar the Horrible") Browne, for example, recently privately published a book depicting forty years of his cards. Walt Kelly loved Christmas and the following pages show his mastery in the variation of different groups of Pogo characters celebrating the holiday. For many Pogophiles, Kelly's art at Christmas is something special.

Most of Kelly's Christmas cards measured 4⅛ x 5½ inches and were printed in two colors on colored 65-pound textured cover stock. The year, where known, and the color combinations used caption the cards reprinted. The reclining Pogo to the left was the front cover of the card below.

Cover: green and red ink with deckle-edged paper; *interior:* green and red ink, textured green cover stock, 1955.

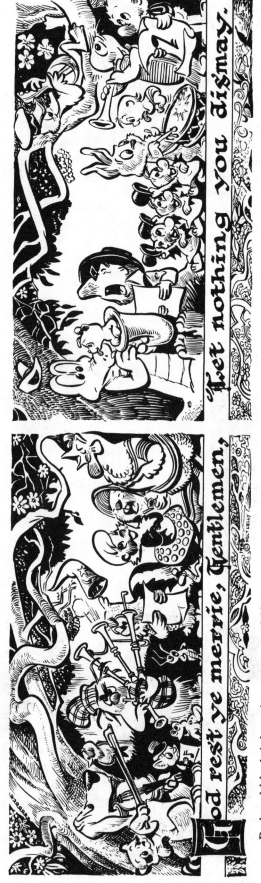

Red and black ink on ivory paper, 1953.

Red and black ink on gray paper, 1954.

Red and black ink on buff paper, 1957.

Red and dark green ink on cream paper, 1958.

Black ink on ivory paper, 1960.

Green ink on gray paper, 1961.

Maroon ink on ivory paper, 1962.

Let nothing you dismay

God rest you merry, Gentlemen

1962 WALT KELLY

Black ink on light blue paper, year unknown.

More Christmas?

MAKE IT MERRY!

WHAT?

In 1966, Walt Kelly kept humor in his Christmas card but thematically took a much more serious stance than his Christmas norm. The phrase "God is not dead. He is merely unemployed." caused a great stir in the press for Pogo.

A MESSAGE...

Blue ink on tan paper, 1966.

A LOOK AT THE POTLOOK THEORY
ON THE ORIGIN OF D.U.A.W.B.C.

Herein the incredible conjecture of Professor Repent Potlook. It should be borne in mind that Jiggs Potlook vigorously belittled this theory, to the point that he retired to a life of counting sugar in Cleveland.

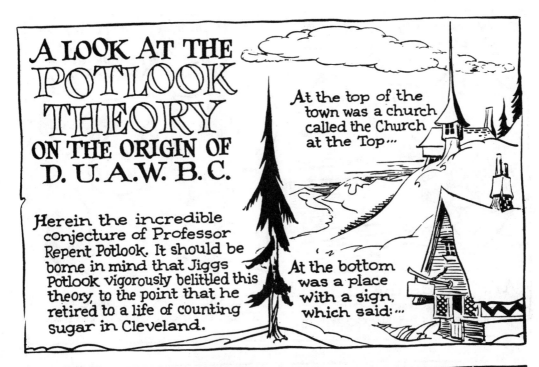

At the top of the town was a church called the Church at the Top ···

At the bottom was a place with a sign, which said: ···

This is the
HADES
(NO TABLES FOR **LADIES**)

And every morning, thru drifts 19 feet deep, there would arrive a sorry apprentice carrying 450 lbs. of coal at exactly 5:00 p.m. on the dot.

And inside the Hades was the kindly old proprietor, Old Nicodemus.

Old Nic always expressed concern about the apprentice.

When, what to his wond'ring
eyes should appear
But a miniature sleigh and
a tiny doll dear…

Hepzibah! That lovely name
Coursed thru his giddy brain
As dry leaves flee the
Hurricane!

Hastily disguising himself
as a choir boy, Nicodemus
hurried up the hill…

He threw open the
choir director's door and
declared himself!

My, what a surprise!

Inside, poor Nicodemus beheld his own apprentice pulling taffy in tandem...

The Choir Director made a startling suggestion.

Torn by a vibrant grief, Nicodemus prudently made exit.

Back at the Hades, Nicodemus tried to drown his sorrow in Peppery Pot.

He thought of hanging ···So he bought a length of rope on credit ···(but decided to not sell tickets).

He decided tying it around his neck would be too painful ··· Nic knotted the noose under his arms and lepped off.

As he fell on his ·· uh ·· floor and was turning around, Down the chimney St. Nicholas came with a bound.

St. Nicholas immediately pointed out the disadvantages of suicide... Nicodemus agreed.

Nic learned that his life-work (spoiling the carols) was a failure...

Then St. Nicholas offered Old Nic a job in the open. Nic accepted! Now when the two

pass over Christmas Choir practice, children's voices waft the beloved carol into the wind.*

*Countless authorities contest this theory

ANTI-MISTLE TOE TO TOE

I always thought
  a Parisite
Was a man who
  lived in France

But beneath
  the mistletoe
I learned who
  wears the pants.

So now I'm
  anti-mistle too,
For, in that
  kissing trance,

I first heard
  that twanging tune,
That tune
  to which I dance.

CHRISTMAS ON THE HARD-SELL

The Whimsical Wham
Of the huckstering
Ham

Who sells
with a slam
The Christmas
calam-

Ity known
as the time
On the air
that is prime

Convinces me I'm
going
out of
my mime!

Bark Us All Bow~Wows of Folly
~ One ~

BUABWOF
~ Two ~

Bark us all bow-wows of folly, Polly wolly cracker 'n' too-da-loo!
Hunky Dory's pop is lolly gaggin' on the wagon, Willy, folly go through!

Donkey bonny brays a carol, antelope cantaloup, 'lope with you!
Chollie's collie barks at Barrow, harum scarum five alarum bung-a-loo!

Xmas
Postludicrosity

This piece may top the list of esoteric Pogo finds amid the Kelly files. Originally published in April 1958 in the News Workshop, published by the Department of Journalism, School of Commerce, Accounts and Finance, New York University, Walt Kelly even drew a wonderful special drawing for his article.

Pogo Learns Human Beans Nothin' At All; Nature's Screechers Just Have Fun

Walt Kelly, Pogo's Papa, admits sociological content of his comic strip, says only real-life situations are found in the Okefenokee swamp

By Robert E. Gerson
from *News Workshop*
Department of Journalism, School of Commerce, Accounts, and Finance,
New York University

"LABELS!" exploded Walt Kelly in his midtown Manhattan office. "Why does everything have to have a label?" The detonator that set off this usually amiable creator of the internationally famous "Pogo" was a question asking if "Pogo" is a sociological comic strip, and if it reflects Kelly's opinions of society.

"I suppose so," was his answer to the question, then he launched into his harangue. "Personally, I like it better when you can enjoy the forest without having to name all the trees."

He said that labels tend to destroy the liberal mind. This forces everything into patterns. He implied that people now expect to have everything explained to them.

"The label," he said, "is almost the opposite of what liberal thought should bring about."

When first syndicated, "Pogo" appeared in just four papers — the New York *Post*, the Philadelphia *Bulletin*, the Washington *Star,* and the Newark *Star-Ledger.* Today, more than five hundred papers carry the strip in their daily or Sunday comic sections.

"I try to keep six to eight weeks ahead in my strips," Kelly said. "Isn't that about where we are now, George?" he asked George Ward, one of his two assistants.

"That's right," George answered.

Neither George, nor Kelly's other assistant, Henry Shikuma, draw any of the "Pogo" strips, Kelly explained. "There is a certain individual quality in 'Pogo,' and I would like to preserve it." He allows Ward to ink in four or five characters over his penciled drawings, but inks all the rest himself.

Pogo's Papa A Doter

KELLY pointed to a panel containing two of Pogo's swamp friends. "You see that line here, and that one there?" he said. "Well, they are exactly the way I want them to be. No one else could do them for me in exactly the same way." Kelly admitted that he may be too much of a perfectionist, but said, "I feel I owe it to the people who have been reading my strip from the beginning." Pogophiles acknowledge the care Kelly takes in his strip and point out that every character from Albert the

Alligator, Pogo's dearest comrade, through Beauregard Bugleboy, whose self-announced loyalty and devotion make him the epitome of dogdom, to the little worm who sticks his head up out of the marshy ground to find out what is going on, has an individual personality all his own.

Kelly, born in Philadelphia in 1913, was whisked to Bridgeport, Connecticut, at the age of two. His father was a theatrical scene painter, and taught Walt to draw. Kelly's newspaper work started at 13, when he worked on a part-time basis for the Bridgeport *Post* as a political cartoonist and high school correspondent. After graduation, he went to work in a garment factory as a floor sweeper. But, not long afterward, he got a job with the Bridgeport paper as a full-time reporter.

Six years later, after a brief uninspiring sojourn in New York, Kelly went west to meet another Walt — Disney. Helping to create such filmed carton classics as "Snow White," "Pinocchio" and "Dumbo," Kelly learned some of the techniques of advanced cartooning.

In 1941, Kelly made a second assault on New York; and this time he made a better showing. While working for a comic book publishing firm, Kelly created a modern fairy tale series called "Bumbazine." Bumbazine was a little boy who lived near a swamp in Georgia called Okefenokee, and his friends were the swamp-dealing creatures. One of the animal characters which

appeared in the series from time to time was a little 'possum named Pogo.

Kelly worked for the army in 1943 as a civilian with a foreign language unit. There, he says, he learned to translate the English language into grammatically correct Georgian. As time went on, more fluent Pogo became more and more important in the series, and eventually replaced the illfated Bumbazine as the leading character.

The rumble of the presses called Kelly back to the profession, and, in 1948, he worked for the New York *Star,* the paper that was supposed to make journalistic history. Kelly took Pogo with him.

On the *Star,* he filled the positions of art director, political cartoonist (with Bill Mauldin), and senior editor. It was Kelly's political cartooning during the 1948 presidential elections that first gave him nationwide attention. His characterization of Dewey as a mechanical man made Kelly famous. "I had Dewey, Truman and Wallace lined up as if at the start of a race," said Kelly, in describing his first mechanical man cartoon. "Wallace ran as a progressive," he stated, "and had been doing strange things — throwing boomerangs, eating flowers and practicing yoga. So I had him running with an arm full of boomerangs. Truman was out running loose, but blindfolded." Dewey, he explained, "was running on a fixed track. He had the body of a slot machine and a tape recorder. The idea grew," he said, "and Dewey became a mechanical man to others."

Any history that the *Star* made had to be made fast, because seven months after the first *Star* came off the press, the paper folded.

At this point there is a hiatus between Kelly's actions as stated by Kelly and his actions as recorded in a brief, humorous biography issued by the Hall Syndicate, Inc., the syndicate handling "Pogo." The Hall biography reads: "After the fold of the *Star* in January 1949, Kelly took the strip to three or four syndicate offices." Kelly says that at the time indicated in the Hall biography, "I offered it no place." An article about Kelly which appeared in the March 8, 1952 issue of *Collier's* states that Kelly offered "Pogo" to several syndicates, but says he made the offer before he joined the *Star.*

The Hall biography says that Kelly "borrowed every nickel he could lay his hands on and took a crosstown bus to the Hall Syndicate" where "we had already had a call from Bob Hall, president of the syndicate," which Kelly says was unlikely because he says that during the *Star*-to-Hall period he was working on a commercial art project, drawing "Pogo" comic books and taking home a substantial paycheck.

Kelly and the Hall biography agree, however, that in May 1949, less than four months after the *Star's* presses had ceased to rumble, Hall called and asked Kelly to

come to the syndicate office. Kelly went, and signed with the syndicate.

Aside from drawing comic strips, Kelly reads them, too. He lists among his favorites such old-timers as "Moon Mullins," "Blondie," "Li'l Abner" and "Dick Tracy." There are some new ones on his list, which now includes "Peanuts," and "Miss Peach." But the strip that is at the very top of his list is "Krazy Kat," which hasn't been run since its creator George Herriman died.

Kelly has an original Herriman cartoon hanging in his office. It was given to him by Herriman's daughter. "I'm not sure that 'Krazy Kat' could really be called a comic strip," Kelly said. There was one thing, however, of which he said he could be sure: "Nobody will ever be as good as he (Herriman) was."

From Pessimists to Optimists
The Swamp Has Them All

Kelly talked about the piece he and author John Lardner once did for *Look*, in which they discussed Herriman and "Krazy Kat." "The editors must have thought we were spelling Herriman's name wrong," he said, "so they changed it to read 'Herman' throughout the story. John," whom Kelly described as his favorite "manipulator of words," "and I have never quite forgiven them for that."

What does Kelly want his strip to do? "Be funny," he said. "I come from a school of old-time cartooning. In the old days, we tried to make a buck out of drawing." Kelly, one of the few cartoonists who owns the copyright to his own strip, implied that the best system for him has always been to be humorous. "I go after whatever seems funny to me," he said.

Everything that you will find in real life you will find in Pogo's section of the Okefenokee Swamp, Kelly stated. Even the dangers are present. His strip has three communist cow birds who feel that everything should be shared, as long as it doesn't belong to them. The swamp has its pessimists, optimists, and at one time even had its own Simple J. McCarthy. "Some things in life are so subtle that I can't get them into the strip," Kelly said. His decisions as to what is or is not too subtle is apparently based on a value judgment. "If I feel that ten percent of the readers will understand what

I am doing, that's fine. If only one percent of them understand an idea, then it's no good."

He said that "Pogo" follows no plot line because plots are not realistic. "The plot is an invention of storytellers." None of Kelly's characters really accomplishes anything or arrives at any conclusions, because "there are no payoffs in life." "Besides," he said, "it always rings untrue when you try to wind up with a specific conclusion."

Kelly's strip is noted for its syllabic aberrations. Pogo's pals refer to themselves as "nature's screechers," and to those whom they are destined to entertain as "human beans." Another Kelly trademark is the alteration of song lyrics. Every Christmas, Pogo and his friends gather to sing such classic carols as "Good King Sauerkraut looked out on his feets uneven," and the ever-popular "Deck us all with Boston Charlie, Walla Walla, Wash., and Kalamazoo." His "Oh, pick a pock of peach pits, pockets full of pie" has caused endless agonies in the "Mother Goose Rhyme" set; while the attack on the "Old West" presented in "Oh, give me a home 'tween Buffalo and Rome, where the beer in the cantalope lay" proves that Kelly holds nothing sacred.

Kelly claims that he just thinks like the characters he draws, and that the phrases and songs come naturally. How do the characters think? "Well," said Kelly, "they think along the line of least resistance, just like water trickling downhill, and following the easiest path."

Pogo — A Possum Without Portfolio

Currently they've launched a "Year of Man" — for with their creator they feel that "we have neglected too long what is under our nose, namely man, in order to study what is essentially over our heads."

When in 1952 and again in 1956, Pogo's friends decided to nominate him for the presidency, thousands of real live people all across the nation rushed to support his platform. Students chanting "I Go Pogo" held rallies and riots on major college campuses. More than 100,000 students proclaimed their loyalty by wearing the Pogo campaign button, and 150 college newspapers officially listed Pogo as their first choice for the presidency. Though Pogo failed to secure the job as chief executive, he has been elected president of several college freshman classes.

Besides giving interviews to professional and semi-professional journalists, turning out daily and Sunday strips, and acting as master of ceremonies at numerous functions, Kelly makes some fifty speeches a year at colleges, professional societies and conventions. He also answers all of his fan mail.

Ten-Twelve Letters A Day
All Get A Prompt Response

"At first, 'Pogo' attracted a lot of mail but now people are used to it." Today he receives from ten to twelve letters a day. Each letter gets a prompt reply and, often, one of the twelve "Pogo" books or an original drawing goes along with the letter.

Kelly was the first comic strip invited to file material with the Library of Congress. However, he had given most of his originals away, and had to go around asking people to give some of them back to him, so he would have something to file.

Simon and Schuster has sold more than two-and-one-half million copies of the "Pogo" books, including one hard cover edition, "Songs of the Pogo," which is a must on the shelf of every music lover. The book contains no less than thirty immortal classics; purists can get eighteen of the songs (three sung by Kelly himself) on a long-playing record.

At the time the Library of Congress accepted "Pogo" for its collection, Duncan Emrich, head of the library's folklore section, said that Kelly "shows great originality, drawing on our basic folk traditions, humor and way of life in the same way that Mark Twain did."

POGO'S PAPA PROMOTES

WALT KELLY often used the phrase "natural born" to describe God-given talent. If he were to describe himself, among his many talents, he certainly was a "natural born promoter." It must be due to the fact he was raised and educated in Bridgeport, Connecticut, home and final resting place of the great showman P. T. Barnum. Of Kelly's contemporaries, only Milton Caniff and Al Capp can hold a candle to him in promotion.

The following news releases are a textbook example of how Kelly and the syndicate kept Pogo in the public eye. Kelly worked hard at it. He constantly gave speeches and traveled to college campuses. He endorsed products, including of all things, concrete.

One of his most brilliant promotions, however, not just for Pogo, but for all cartoonists, was a trip to the White House made by the National Cartoonists Society. In the early 1950s, when cartooning and comic books were under fire from the self-rightous right, Kelly led his fellow cartoonists directly into Ike's office. Caricatures and text from the book resulting from that Oval Office visitation are reprinted.

The HALL Syndicate, Inc.

342 MADISON AVENUE · NEW YORK 17, N. Y.

ROBERT M. HALL
President

MUrray Hill 2-5560

December 3, 1954

Dear Editor:

In the activities of POGO's creator, there is often grist
for your promotion of the feature. We think you'll find the following
particularly interesting and useful.

Walt Kelly will join the popular Dumont Network TV panel
program, "Down You Go" Dec. 8 and Dec. 15 as a regular panel member.
This program, one of TV's most popular and longest-lived guessing
games, is telecast widely throughout the country and almost certainly
appears in your area. In New York "Down You Go" appears at 10 p.m.
Wednesdays on Channel 5 -- live.

On Dec. 12, Walt Kelly will make a one-shot appearance on
"Look Up and Live" ---- at 10:30 a.m. Sunday over Channel 2 in New York
City, at other times over other stations in the network. This same
show will appear one week later, Dec. 19, in Los Angeles; two weeks
later, Dec. 26, in Galveston, Memphis and San Francisco.

Original POGO material is on exhibit at the Library of
Congress, South Hall, Main Building, from Dec. 6 through January 15.

We trust these memos will be helpful to you or your promotion director. The TV programs will give readers, who are tremen-
dously interested in POGO and its creator, an opportunity to meet on
the screen this gifted and effective humorist.

Sincerely,

Robert M. Hall

From: The Hall Syndicate, Inc.
        342 Madison Avenue
        New York 17, N.Y.

FOR IMMEDIATE RELEASE

World Brotherhood has selected Pogo's papa, Walt Kelly, as master-of-ceremonies for its annual dinner on Feb. 17 to honor four winners of a global essay contest. The dinner, at International House, Columbia University, is a highlight of Brotherhood Week, Feb. 16-23.

The contest winners — a Burmese housewife, a police instructor from Ghana, a Danish Army officer and a student from Mexico — were chosen from among thousands of entries from 108 nations and protectorates, including Russia and her satellites. The contest, announced during November by the World Wide English Service of the Voice of America, called for a 200-word essay in English on "What World Brotherhood Means to Me."

Walt Kelly, creator of the famous Pogo comic strip, which appears in over 500 newspapers in the United States and abroad, is a former two-term president of the National Cartoonists Society and a winner of the coveted "Cartoonist of the Year" award. He is the author of 13 books. Kelly recently returned from a round-the-world trip — his second in two years — during which he addressed cultural groups and gathered material for a new book, "Not So Square a World," to be published in the fall. A much sought-after public speaker, he is a particular favorite of college student and faculty audiences. During his annual swing of campuses this spring, he will speak at ten colleges.

"The selection of Walt Kelly as master-of-ceremonies for the Feb. 17 dinner is a happy one for us," Dr. Everett R. Clinchy, president of World Brotherhood, said. "His work through the medium of the comic strip is a valuable contribution to greater understanding of the problems of living together and helping one another as civilized neighbors. As an artist, a humorist and a world traveler, Mr. Kelly has worked toward many of the same goals as the Brotherhood. The wide popularity of his strip is evidence of how effectively he has done his daily job as one individual interested in good-will and brotherhood."

From: The Hall Syndicate, Inc.
342 Madison Avenue
New York 17, New York

FACT SHEET: Incidents & Statistics in the Life of Pogo & Walt Kelly

The Pogo comic strip is carried by 507 daily and Sunday newspapers in the United States and abroad.

As of January, 1958, there have been 12 Pogo books published (Simon & Schuster), with sales of more than 2,400,000. Walt Kelly has also published "Songs of the Pogo," a book containing 30 original songs and music, plus a long-playing record of 18 of the songs; he has also done the illustrations for six other books.

When the U.S. Department of Labor needed a symbol in the fall of 1957 to dramatize its manpower campaign ("Stay in School and Graduate"), it chose Pogo. Pogo appeared in all media: newspapers, radio, television, posters, stickers, etc. During the campaign, Pogo appeared 7,560 times on TV throughout the country, and extolled the advantages of a high school diploma in a Kelly-drawn Department of Labor editorial cartoon carried by 600 newspapers.

When the U.S. Treasury Department needed help in getting its Savings Bonds message across, Pogo and Walt Kelly moved in and reached more readers of factory, labor and trade publications than any other comic strip specially drawn for the campaign.

When the Library of Congress decided to set up a permanent collection of outstanding American comic strip art, it initiated the project with a collection of original Pogo strips.

When the nation's college campuses got into the Presidential election swing in 1956, more than 100,000 students wore I GO POGO buttons; 156 student newspapers officially endorsed Pogo as first choice for the White House. (Pogo was even elected president of several college freshman classes!) And the American Heritage Foundation used his services to help get out the vote nationally.

When Life magazine decided to do a job on Asiatic flu, it called on Pogo to help convince its readership that caution and common sense, not panic, was the answer.

Walt Kelly makes about 50 speeches each year, talking and sketching before college student and faculty groups, hospital patients, professional societies, conventions, etc.

Pogo's creator has circled the globe twice. His most recent round-the-world trip was spent addressing cultural groups and gathering material for a new book.

Walt Kelly is a former two-term president of the National Cartoonists Society and a winner of the "Cartoonist of the Year" award. In 1947 he won the Heywood Broun Memorial Award for the best editorial cartoon of the year.

From The Hall Syndicate, Inc.
    342 Madison Avenue, New York 17, N.Y.

FOR RELEASE JUNE 4 and thereafter.

NEW YORK, June 4—Rochester, New York, and Worthington, Minnesota, 1958 winners of the World Brotherhood Community Awards for promoting international understanding, have been cited by the Committee for the Year of Man for "giving impetus to our common move toward the celebration of mankind."

The citation, an illuminated scroll designed by Walt Kelly, creator of the Pogo comic strip, was presented last night to representatives of the City of Worthington by Philippine Ambassador Carlos P. Romulo and Mr. Kelly during World Brotherhood Award ceremonies at the World Affairs Center of the Carnegie Endowment Building here. The presentation to Rochester will be made there today by General Romulo when that city celebrates its achievements in the field of world understanding and friendship.

The Year of Man scroll, signed by Pogo and other animal characters who people the Kelly strip, concludes: "And so it is that the Committee for the Year of Man joins the people of Rochester (and Worthington) and the World in hoping that one fair day we may all be completely human, sure in the knowledge that it is this dream which makes us all akin."

    Text of the scroll:

"Whereas, in this eighteen-months-long G.O. Fizzickle Year of the Scientist, the Good People of the City of Rochester and Worthington have opened their Eyes, their Minds and their Hands to All Others in this Not-So-Square World;

"And Whereas, these Kind and Gentle People have made a decision to explore the Inner Space of Man and leave Outer Space to its own Imperfect Emptiness, unmarred save by the Drifting of Clockwork Moons;

"And Whereas, They have sown the Gold, the Frankincense and the Myrrh of Love upon the Troubled Waters of the Earth;

"Therefore, We, whose Names appear below, having formed a Committee for the Year of Man, a never-ending Year devoted to the Study of Inner Space and the Firm Holding of Hands, do hereby Hail and Honor each of the Citizens of This Fair City for giving impetus to our Common Move toward the Celebration of Mankind.

"And so it is that the Committee for the Year of Man joins the People of Rochester (and Worthington) and the World in hoping that One Fair Day we may all be Completely Human, sure in the Knowledge that it is this Dream which makes us all akin."

From Post—Hall Syndicate, Inc.
    342 Madison Avenue, New York 17, N.Y.

FOR IMMEDIATE RELEASE

Walt Kelly, creator of POGO, made presentation Tuesday to President Eisenhower of a volume of 95 cartoons of the President by as many artists of the National Cartoonists Society.

The presentation was made in the name of the Cartoonists as a souvenir of the Society's breakfast with Eisenhower last June, when the cartoons were drawn. Kelly, who is now president of the National Cartoonists Society, was accompanied to the White House by three past presidents, Alex Raymond, Milt Caniff, and Rube Goldberg.

Also present at the ceremonies were Secretary of the Treasury George Humphrey, Earl O. Shreve, National Director, Savings Bond Division and other Treasury officials.

From The Hall Syndicate, Inc.
342 Madison Avenue, New York 17, New York.

FOR IMMEDIATE RELEASE

Walt Kelly, creator of Pogo and author of 14 books featuring his famous comic strip character, has been selected as one of the judges of the 1958 National Book Awards. He will serve on a five-man panel to choose the "most distinguished" book of non-fiction published this year.

Selection of Kelly marks the first time in its ten years that the National Book Awards Committee has named an artist to its judges board. Serving with him will be Catherine Drinker Bowen, author; Huntington Cairns, lawyer and author; Thomas H. Johnson, teacher and editor; and Gerard Piel, magazine publisher.

The awards, including selections in the fields of fiction and poetry, will be made in New York City on March 3, 1959. They are the only industry-wide honors in the book publishing field and are sponsored by the American Book Publishers Council, the American Booksellers Association and the Book Manufacturers' Institute.

Walt Kelly's Pogo books have topped sales of $2\frac{1}{2}$ million, and his writings, as well as his art, have appeared in most of the major magazines. Kelly is also in wide demand as a public speaker, making 40-50 addresses each year before college, business, press and civic organizations. His comic strip, appearing in 519 newspapers with a circulation of 44,560,000 is distributed by the Hall Syndicate.

####

PRESIDENTIAL PROMOTION

From Post-Hall Syndicate, Inc.
   342 Madison Avenue, New York 17, N.Y.

FOR IMMEDIATE RELEASE

Walt Kelly, creator of Pogo and author of 14 books featuring his famous comic strip character, has been selected as one of the judges of the 1958 National Book Awards. He will serve on a five-man panel to choose the "most distinguished" book of non-fiction published this year.

Selection of Kelly marks the first time in its ten years that the National Book Awards Committee has named an artist to its judges board. Serving with him will be Catherine Drinker Bowen, author; Huntington Cairns, lawyer and author; Thomas H. Johnson, teacher and editor; and Gerard Piel, magazine publisher.

The awards, including selections in the fields of fiction and poetry, will be made in New York City on March 3, 1959. They are the only industry-wide honors in the book publishing field and are sponsored by the American Book Publishers Council, the American Booksellers Association and the Book Manufacturers' Institute. Walt Kelly's Pogo books have topped sales of 2½ million, and his writings, as well as his art, have appeared in most of the major magazines. Kelly is also in wide demand as a public speaker, making 40-50 addresses each year before college, business, press and civic organizations. His comic strip, appearing in 519 newspapers with a circulation of 44,560,000 is distributed by the Hall Syndicate.

INTRODUCTION

☆ ☆ ☆ ☆ ☆ ☆ ☆ ☆ ☆ ☆ ☆ ☆ ☆

IN JUNE, 1954, President Eisenhower met with members of the National Cartoonists Society in Washington. The Society, composed of men and women who are considered to be among the foremost exponents of the cartoonist's art in the nation, wished to confer honorary membership upon one of the few Presidents since Thomas Jefferson who has evidenced and exercised any talents as an artist. By this action, the cartoonists reaffirmed their support of the United States Savings Bonds Program.

It is a matter of interest that many comic-strip creators have followings of fans as widespread and numerous as those of any movie performer, TV or radio personality, or sports star. Moreover, to a vast public their creations have transcended paper and ink and have become as real as any characters in literature or on the stage. Morale officers at service centers attest that the creators of popular story-strips and cartoon series are often received as enthusiastically as stage or screen performers. The President's meeting with the artists was a recognition of their services in promoting the sale of Savings Bonds since the inception on May 1, 1941, of the Series E Bonds Program.

WALT KELLY...Walt Kelly's *Pogo* the Possum, Albert the Alligator and other Okefenokee Swamp characters have enjoyed a popularity among the intelligentsia comparable to, but more meteoric than, George Herriman's *Krazy Kat*. Kelly is an ex-president of the National Cartoonists Society.

WITH GREAT RESPECT & ADMIRATION, WALT KELLY

" IN CASE YOU AIN'T ALREADY GOT A ALLIGATOR IN THE CABINET, MR. PRESIDENT, I KNOW A BOY WHO IS AVAILABLE -- "

Also, it was incidental recognition that in the United States of America the press is a Fourth Estate in fact, with an acknowledged position as a formulator and molder of public opinion, and with the right of direct access to the Chief Executive. The President's regular practice of responding to spontaneous questions from newspaper and radio representatives on the Executive's actions and policies, and of permitting on some occasions public broadcasts and telecasts of these searching examinations, has no parallel in any other major nation. It is perhaps the closest practical approach to democracy possible in a country of 160,000,000 people.

By now the Presidential press conference is an established custom. However, there was no precedent for President Eisenhower's similarly placing himself before a gathering of newspaper and magazine artists for their free use of him as a subject for portrait, caricature, gag cartoon, or illustration.

The occasion took the form of a breakfast. While the courses were being served and exchanges of talk were going on, artists had free hands with drawing paper or board, pencil or pen. When Mr. Eisenhower had concluded his formal remarks, in which he urged the cartoonists to continue to use their medium to teach the youth of the nation "truth, honor and, above all, dedication," he asked to see the drawings made of him. He smiled broadly as one after another was held up, and laughed outright at some of the gags. "Don't cheat on me! I want them," he exclaimed.

In fulfillment of this request, the National Cartoonists Society collected the originals of the 95 drawings made on that occasion in a large leather-bound volume designed by Frank Fogarty and sent it to the White House.

When the story and pictures of the presentation of the volume to the President appeared in newspapers all over the country, book publisher Frederick Fell in New York City was moved by the thought that this was the only country in which a representative group of its cartoonists could sit down to breakfast with the Chief of State and have the freedom to portray him, caricature him, lampoon him, as they wished. It was, Mr. Fell thought, a graphic manifestation of what makes this country worth fighting for and its government a good investment. He wrote to the

President suggesting that publication of the cartoons in book form could be a further means of aiding the Savings Bonds Program to which the cartoonists had given their talent and time. Mr. Fell said: "As a publisher the thought occurred to me that the country at large would be most interested in seeing the various sketches of you as made by the leading cartoonists in the country and that such a book, published in connection with the Savings Bonds Program, would be a most effective way of giving increased impetus to this program." Mr. Fell then offered the facilities of his publishing house for the purpose, as a public service.

A prompt reply was received from the White House. The President declared the proposal "a very interesting one," and referred it to Secretary of the Treasury George M. Humphrey. This was followed by a letter from Mr. Humphrey, giving his approval to the project. His letter constitutes the foreword to this volume.

After necessary permissions had been obtained from the artists, production work was delayed by the President's illness, inasmuch as the originals were in the White House. Among the letters President Eisenhower wrote soon after his recovery is the one reproduced in this book. It was delivered to the publisher with the album itself after Mr. Eisenhower returned to Washington. This is typical of the President's devotion to the Savings Bonds Program.

President Eisenhower has consistently urged all Americans to buy United States Savings Bonds to protect their own and their nation's security. He has said that the government bond program gives "every individual and every family a chance at the opportunities and happiness that go with financial independence. It enables every citizen to save on a safe and systematic basis, and thereby to contribute to the economic stability of his community and the nation."

This book would not have been possible without the gracious consent of President Dwight D. Eisenhower; the co-operation of Secretary of the Treasury George M. Humphrey, and the enthusiastic and unanimous consent of the participating members of the National Cartoonists Society to the publication of their work.

Thanks and appreciation are also expressed to James C. Hagerty, Press Secretary to the President; Nils A. Lennartson, Assistant to the Secretary of the Treasury; Leon Siler, Information Officer of the Treasury Department; and Ann C. Whitman, Personal Secretary to the President.

Also to Alex Raymond, National Affairs Secretary of the National Cartoonists Society; Marge Duffy Devine, Scribe of the National Cartoonists Society; and Clark Kinnaird.

All profits derived from the original publication of this volume and all authors' royalties have been waived in favor of the widest dissemination of this volume and the United States Savings Bonds message it contains.

—The Publishers

☆ ☆ ☆ ☆ ☆ ☆ ☆ ☆ ☆ ☆ ☆ ☆ ☆

Photo (left to right): Milton Caniff, creator of STEVE CANYON; Alex Raymond, creator of RIP KIRBY; W. Randolph Burgess, Under Secretary of the Treasury; President Dwight D. Eisenhower; Earl O. Shreve, National Director of Savings Bonds Division; Walt Kelly, creator of POGO and President of the National Cartoonists Society; Rube Goldberg, editorial cartoonist, Hearst papers; and Secretary of the Treasury George M. Humphrey, during presentation of a bound volume of 95 cartoons of the President at the White House — January 3, 1955

WAYNE BORING currently draws the newspaper version of *Superman*, in which a troop of artists and writers have had a hand since it was originated by Jerry Siegel and Joe Schuster. They brought it out in 1938, after *Buck Rogers*, *Flash Gordon* and other strips had created a new wave of popularity for pictorial fantasy fiction.

GILL FOX, who first won notice with cartoons in the *Washington Daily News*, is the artist of the strip *Wilbert* for General Features Corporation.

MURAT "CHIC" YOUNG . . . Chic Young's contribution deserves a prominent place in any album of great cartoonists. No other comic strip ever attained the world-wide popularity of his *Blondie*, which he started for King Features Syndicate in 1930. "Dagwood" and "sandwich" are synonymous in a dozen languages.

GUS EDSON took over *The Gumps* comic strip after Sydney Smith died. As stated in a previous note, he collaborates with Irwin Hasen on another strip, *Dondi*. Edson is a vice-president of the National Cartoonists Society.

L. D. WARREN . . . Warren gave sharp focus to his caricature of the President by use of bold strokes in the same master manner employed by A. Hirschfeld. Warren is editorial cartoonist for the *Cincinnati Enquirer*.

TO PRESIDENT DWIGHT D. EISENHOWER WITH BEST WISHES
L D WARREN
CINCINNATI ENQUIRER.

DWIGHT D EISENHOWER

TO THE PRESIDENT WITH SINCERE ADMIRATION — ALEX RAYMOND

ALEX RAYMOND . . . Alexander Gillespie Raymond, an illustrator of high talents, has made his drawing of the *Rip Kirby* story strip a work of art in a real sense. It is his second memorable creation, the first having been the *Flash Gordon* Sunday fantasy pages. For some years he also drew the *Secret Agent X-9* daily strips.

Bill Crawford
NEWARK NEWS

BILL CRAWFORD is the editorial cartoonist of the *Newark Evening News*, an artist whose wit and technical skills make him one of the best of contemporary practitioners in his field. His political commentaries are regularly picked up by other newspapers.

MILTON CANIFF . . . The contributor of this outstanding portrait put on paper two enormously popular pictorial novels. After having made *Terry and the Pirates* the best drawn, best written and most exciting story strip up to that time, Caniff abandoned it to launch *Steve Canyon*. In the latter he has overcome the narrow limitations of newspaper-strip space and form with his remarkably brilliant dialogue and subtle character shading.

WELCOME MR. PRESIDENT-- TO THE NATIONAL CARTOONISTS SOCIETY.

With very best wishes

WILSON McCOY

WILSON McCOY is the artist half of the team responsible for the King Features Syndicate daily and Sunday strip *The Phantom*. It is written by Lee Falk, who doubles as author of the strip *Mandrake the Magician*.

CAVU & BEST WISHES TO OUR ARTIST-PILOT-PRESIDENT, SMILIN' IKE, FROM SMILIN' JACK

& ZACK MOSLEY

ZACK MOSLEY... Mosley mixed up aviation, sex, and villainy with notable success in the strip, *Smilin' Jack*, for the Chicago Tribune-New York News Syndicate. He qualified as an authority on at least one of these, through long experience as a pilot.

HIGH SPOTS IN A YOUNG CARTOONIST'S LIFE

GOSH! I'M A MEMBER OF THE NATIONAL CARTOONISTS SOCIETY! I COULDN'T BE HAPPIER IF I WERE THE PRESIDENT OF THE UNITED STATES!

IRWIN HASEN

IRWIN HASEN contributes gag cartoons to national magazines. In addition, he collaborates with Gus Edson on the new strip, *Dondi*, for the Chicago Tribune-New York News Syndicate.

ALAS.. CAN I FIND **NO** PROFESSION WITHOUT ITS OCCUPATIONAL HAZARDS?

EISENHOWER ACRES

DARRELL McCLURE

DARRELL McCLURE draws that perpetual youngster, *Little Annie Rooney*, for King Features Syndicate. Such is her winsome appeal that thousands of persons have been moved to send cards and gifts to the fictional Annie by the mere mention of her birthday.

PRODUCT ENDORSEMENTS

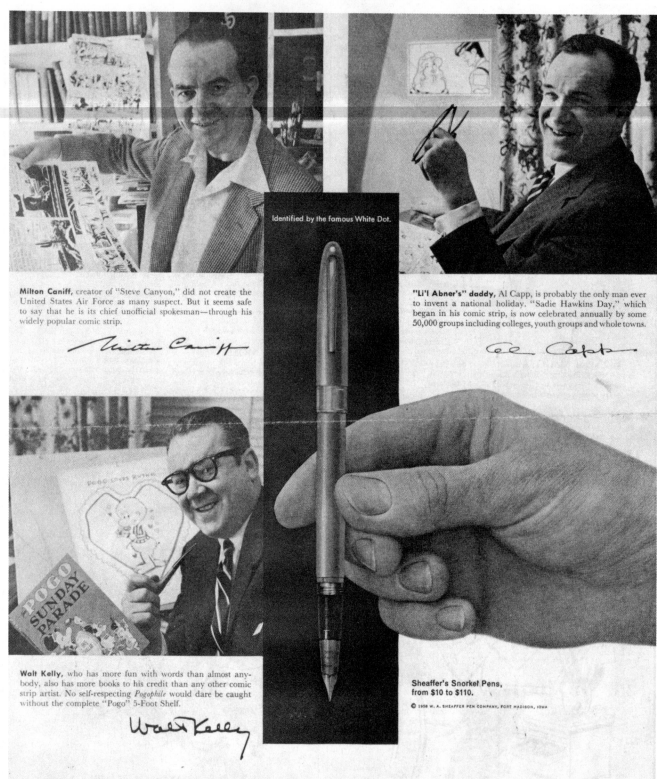

Identified by the famous White Dot.

Milton Caniff, creator of "Steve Canyon," did not create the United States Air Force as many suspect. But it seems safe to say that he is its chief unofficial spokesman—through his widely popular comic strip.

Milton Caniff

"Li'l Abner's" daddy, Al Capp, is probably the only man ever to invent a national holiday. "Sadie Hawkins Day," which began in his comic strip, is now celebrated annually by some 50,000 groups including colleges, youth groups and whole towns.

Al Capp

Walt Kelly, who has more fun with words than almost anybody, also has more books to his credit than any other comic strip artist. No self-respecting *Pogophile* would dare be caught without the complete "Pogo" 5-Foot Shelf.

Walt Kelly

Sheaffer's Snorkel Pens,
from $10 to $110.

© 1958 W. A. SHEAFFER PEN COMPANY, FORT MADISON, IOWA

The more important the signature, the more likely you'll find it is written with the world's finest writing instrument, the distinguished Sheaffer Snorkel Fountain Pen.

Interstate 44 (also U.S. 66) bypassing St. Louis, Missouri—another new-type concrete highway

"Highways should be seen and not heard! So make mine new-type concrete!"

Says **WALT KELLY**,

famous cartoonist, creator of the

popular comic strip, "Pogo"

New route numbers for Interstate Highways! You'll follow specially numbered red, white and blue markers, and you'll find all East-West highways have *even* numbers and all North-South highways have *odd* numbers.

NEW-TYPE
Concrete

"I go concrete—new-type concrete—every time I can. Believe me, it rides as smooth as it looks. This pavement's really flat. No dips and humps. And no thumps either. Mighty quiet and relaxing —the way I like it. We're going to see a lot of this concrete on the new Interstate System, much to my pleasure!"

How smooth a ride can you get? Head your car onto a highway of *new-type concrete!* You'll see . . . and marvel! You glide along . . . and so quietly.

With new-type concrete, highway engineers have put under your wheels the flattest pavement there is. Specially designed subbases will keep it that way for you an expected *50 years and more.*

Even freezing and de-icers won't roughen that beautiful surface. A remarkable process called "air entrainment" puts billions of tiny air bubbles into the concrete and prevents this.

There are no thumps. Most new-type concrete is continuous-laid with only tiny, sawed-in cushion spaces you can't *hear* or *feel*. It's *sound-conditioned* —and your restful ride proves it!

And concrete fits today's emphasis on safety. Its grainy surface provides real skid resistance— even when wet. At night, concrete helps you see better. Its clean, bright color reflects far more light than any dark surface.

Concrete stretches your tax dollars, too! First cost is moderate. Upkeep will be low—as much as 60% lower than for asphalt. That's why new-type concrete is the preferred pavement for America's new Interstate System.

PORTLAND CEMENT ASSOCIATION

A national organization to improve and extend the uses of concrete

Walt Kelly Views the Press with CBS-TV

On Sunday, July 15, 1962, between 4:45-5:00 P.M., Walt Kelly appeared on the WCBS-TV public affairs program, "CBS-TV Views the Press." The transcript of the Kelly segment of the show has not been reset into type so you can enjoy the format where the visuals are listed on the left to accompany the text on the right. Some Pogo strips showing the characters discussed illustrate this piece.

Walt Kelly
15 July 1962

WCBS-TV VIEWS THE PRESS

CALMER:

This is Ned Calmer. During the vacation period, WCBS-TV Views the Press is presenting a series of guest critics noted in their individual fields of activity. Today, Walt Kelly, in a discussion of the problems peculiar to the world of the political cartoon and the comic strip. Mr. Kelly.

KELLY:

Satire in the hands of most cartoonists, including this one, becomes at best, sarcasm; at worst, ridicule. This is especially true of editorial cartooning, but it is also true of the comic strip where pathos, buffoonery and unadulterated malarkey make up the daily grist. On occasion, we come close to satire through parody which is merely broad caricature both in words and in picture.

PIG ON DRAWING BOARD

Ten Everlovin' Blue-eyed Years with POGO

Thus, being a parodist and buffoon, I was surprised recently to find the cartoon of the pig here accused of being satire in bad taste. Also, POGO was accused of having gone in for editorial comment and of making fun of politics. The accusers were editors of a few papers carrying POGO, who thought they saw in the pig some resemblance to a head of state. If editorial comment, whether on social themes or political, is ruled not part of comic strips, it may account for the low level of entertainment seemingly demanded by the objecting editors. If politics is not a matter of fun, what's the use of the practice? All of us,

BB-Journal-American, June 25
LA-Comic Art in America,
    p. 186 by Steve Becker
TP-Comic Art, p. 203

including Mort Walker with his BEETLE BAILEY, Al
Capp with LI'L ABNER, Milt Caniff through TERRY AND
THE PIRATES and then his present strip STEVE CANYON
have at one time or another punctured the balloons
of pomposity. We might come close to parody, perhaps
unwittingly, in our search for fun, but satire is
beyond us. When you deal with fifty-million readers
every day you don't monkey around too much with
subtlety, especially in the space provided for
strips these days, and it must be remembered that
satire is a subtle science. Nothing that we have
done reminds me in the least of Anatole France's
PENGUIN ISLAND, nor of the Reverend Dodgson's ALICE
IN WONDERLAND.

Comic Art, p. 12

It is true that we are a far distance from THE
YELLOW KID, which in 1893 started the fad for regular
comic material in newspapers. In cartoons of the
era, racial gags were thought best for the hilarity
which insured healthy circulations. Today we are a
little more specific. We pick on traits of the

Comic Art, p. 188

individual. The mushminded SENATOR PHOGBOUND in
Li'L Abner; and then the brassbound egomania of a

Journal-American, June 29

General Officer in BEETLE BAILEY; the brainless

N. Y. Post, June 27, p. 45

narcissism of occasional caricatures in JULES FEIFFER's

Pogo Strip

strip; or the backwoods prowl of a Wiley Catt or a

Everlovin' Years, p. 139

Simple J. Malarkey. We know now that the assured

Comic Art

butt of a joke is not an Irishman, as it was at the
turn of the century (IRISH CARTOON), nor a Negro,
nor a Jew.

Some may conclude that we cartoonists have been
limited by edicts on subject matter, but the fact is
that the world has grown up a little. We now know
that every man is funny and that the depths of humor
lie within oneself. On the other hand, as the
NATIONAL CARTOONIST SOCIETY recently lamented, the
appreciation of some readers and some editors seems
to be limited according to whom you are funny against.
Politicians, for example, are not convulsed when
you make fun of something which they are for, either
because they fundamentally approve of the subject or
for reasons of political expediency.

Recently in Tokyo, sharp-eyed Soviet Embassy officials,
evidently avid comic-strip readers, remained in a
state of puzzlement throughout the week of the first
running of POGO strips containing the aforementioned

Pogo Strip

Pig and a Goat companion which some thought resembled
another more or less world figure.

At last, presumably galvanized into action, one of
their number rushed to Mr. Shiba, the editor of the
Asahi Evening News, the Tokyo paper in which POGO
normally appears. The pig, who is as yet unlabeled
and has never been identified by me, was described

to Mr. Shiba as bearing an unfortunate resemblance to
an important head of state.

Mr. Shiba, to give him credit for editorial delibera-
tion, left the matter of any intentional or accidental
resemblance up to his board of directors. After a
solemn conclave, the directors, three days later,
reported back that there did seem to be some likeness
between the pig and the head of state. Mr. Shiba said:
"Therefore, we have decided to discontinue use of the
pig while the resemblance exists." The Tokyo paper
added that the Japanese are very sensitive about the
Emperor, will not condone his being lampooned and
feel the same way about other heads of state. However,
Mr. Shiba disclaimed any opinion as to whether a
resemblance existed. "I don't understand POGO anyway,"
he said. Some of this confusion may be explained by
the translated name of the ASAHI EVENING NEWS. It
means the MORNING EVENING NEWS.

The strips containing the pig and the goat, by the
time of the drop, had appeared in the Tokyo paper for
eleven days or long enough to have any fancied
insults to a foreign power discovered by sheer
editorial skill. However, the paper wanted it made
clear that pressure from the Soviet government was
in no way involved.

Long as that action took, it took the AP story from
Tokyo to alert Canadian papers to the fact that pigs
and goats were in the funnies. Upon verification of
this, several newspapers suspended the strip. One
paper, The Vancouver Sun, canceled entirely claiming
that the strips were in "bad taste." Thoroughly
aroused Canadian readers later clipped the Sun's front
page which showed disrobing Doukhober ladies protesting a political measure. The clips were sent to me
and I was asked which was in worse taste. Except
that I do not think pigs are intentionally nude and
never in bad taste, I have no comment.

The reason that the Doukhober ladies of Western
Canada were reverting to their traditional means of
protest was that the Canadians were in the midst of
an election campaign and the ladies were definitely
against one thing or another. It is possible that
the newspapers which denuded themselves in the
comic strip business were protesting against what
they thought was a sly dig at the continuance of
Canadian trade with Cuba and China, both allegedly
Communist countries. This trade, in a time of
declining Canadian dollar values, is heatedly defended
by politicians of one side and attacked by others.
There is a real confusion in the minds of the public
about which is right or wrong, to trade or not to
trade.

Though not intended as such, the coincidental dig by the POGO strip evidently hit a sensitive nerve.

Pogo Strip, May 14, NYP

It is true that one strip for May 14th showed the goat inquiring about a counterfeit trading stamp deal which the Pig hoped would upset the American 'Ecomedy." "This will do this?" asked the goat, "upset the Kennedyian Apple Core?" Then unable to resist a play on words, I had the pig reply: "Not CANADIAN, U. S. APPLE CART." This convulsed me and I let it stay. However, I apologize now, not for the sentiment, but the joke. I had no idea it would arouse Canada, but I have not heard from President Kennedy. He is evidently a busy man.

My hat is off to the alert Soviet official in Tokyo, he of the Freudian eye. He certainly got the pig a lot of unexpected publicity and is especially to be commended by the HALL SYNDICATE which sent out advance notices of the impending sequence involving pigs and goats to over 600 newspapers carrying POGO throughout the world. The Soviet official was the only one we are sure of who did not get an advance look at the dire implications some unkind eyes have read into the harmless fun of a swamp idyll. Yet it was he who sounded the alarm. Bully!

Mr. Dan Nicoll of the Toledo Blade was the only man to protest before the fact. He declined to use the pig and goat series, having looked at the advance

releases. He said, "The reason for this action on

our part is that we do not wish to run any comic strip

which has as its main topic, directly or indirectly,

anything which has to do with politics." Mr. Nicoll

added that he hoped to have the strip back when it was

"normal." It should be noted here that normalcy in

Simple J. Malarkey -   POGO has included Simple J. Malarkey, whom many took to
   Everlovin' Yrs., p. 139

                                      be a mid-west Senator in the mid-fifties; an owl who

Owl - Everlovin' Yrs., p.253   spoke in the stammering rhythms of a President of the

United States; a speakeasy school for all children

in Virginia who were barred from attendance because the

State felt it should close all schools to stave off

the perils of segregation; and recently the Rightist

Jack Acid Society Book by   Jack Acid Society which was an outright attack on all
   Walt Kelly

Vigilante committees.

Efforts by the Toronto Globe and Mail to stifle the

protests of many readers against the suspension of

the strip did not have the desired result. The Globe

and Mail reprinted POGO strips from years back. The

readers continued to protest. It is fairly evident

that the reading public wants to know what we have

done today which is additionally foolish and witless.

Yesterday's humor is like yesterday's newspaper.

It should be made clear that to leave out treatment

of political themes would be to ignore a mine of

comic material so vast that it has at this point

merely had its surface sounded with a Geiger counter.
So it is Mr. Nicoll's duty, or the duty of any editor,
to not run material if he so chooses, such material
as comment on government, near-government and neo-
government, and so it is the privilege, the right
and the duty of all cartoonists to not run from
making that comment.

It is interesting that I have been advised by Mr.
Robert Hall of the Hall Syndicate, who distributes
POGO throughout the world, to continue to find my fun
wherever it exists and to use it. "You'll help
revive an otherwise spiritless comic-strip industry,"
was his somewhat prejudiced remark.

TIME Magazine, Press   As TIME Magazine recently inferred, editors feel that
Section, May 25
                              comments such as POGO makes "...trespass on the
                              editorial writer's preserve." TIME may be right
                              about how editors feel, but I cannot agree that such
                              comment is not funny, nor that it does not belong in
                              a comic strip.

                              Approximately 610 editors must have agreed with this
                              conclusion for not more than a half-dozen suspended
                              the strip. In fact, the New York POST commented
                              editorially that it looked as if POGO was being once
                              again the brash little possum we have come to admire.
                              The PEORIA JOURNAL STAR said in an editorial: "A
                              story on 'Russian co-operation' today said that the

PEORIA JOURNAL STAR, June 6

U. S. and Russia were close to agreement on a co-
ordinated space research program. Russia is going
to do us a favor. But on the comics page POGO is
illustrating what happens when some people do favors
for you." The JOURNAL STAR then showed a panel from
the strip wherein the turtle, Churchie La Femme, is
talking to the Pig. He says: "Last time you did us
a favor some of us was out of the hospital in only
a coupla days." The publisher, Henry P. Slane, then
remarked rather glumly: "...the Soviets have talked
cooperation before, and every time they did, we got
hurt."

The Okinawa MORNING STAR had a solution to the Tokyo
ban. In a page one editorial it said: "If Pogo were
of a political nature, he might charge the Soviets
with interference in the domestic affairs of Japan.
He would be right, too.

"Our solution to the Soviet assault on the POGO fans
of Japan is to rush to their aid. Five-hundred
copies of the MORNING STARcontaining Pogo sequences
were printed and were rushed to Tokyo by air. In
Tokyo they will be given free distribution through
the Foreign Correspondents Club, an institution
which has long been one of Japan's outstanding
cultural oases."

When we get into the question of why newspapers run
comic strips in the first place, we must go back to

the days, beginning at about the turn of the century
when big newspapers first came into being. Illustrated
comic art and the fast rotary press went hand-in-hand.
The press wars between Mr. Hearst and Mr. Pulitzer are
history and each employed the comic strip to attract
customers. As we have remarked here, the easy gag then
was one which employed the quick or external laugh.
It was then, and is now, easy to make fun of the
outsider. Now we must make fun of ourselves. We
know that we as much as anybody are the real culprits.
Therefore, the present-day working cartoonist, if
he is aware of the world around him, realizes that
within himself are all the seeds of happiness,
laughter, destruction or guilt. So he searches himself.
No longer do we go for the joke which is at the
expense of someone else.

This great book, COMIC ART IN AMERICA by Steve Becker,
published by Simon and Schuster, contains a fine yet
mild history of where we have gone in the newspaper
cartoon business. From a creature that merely served
the publisher as a circulation booster, we find comic
strips taking on more significance.

It is impossible in these days to lay down the rule
that comics must be innocuous. They must be vibrant
and of our time. The easy slapstick gag has lost its

savor. The incredible cliffhanger has left its

charm with the television adventure stories. These

are days when the cartoonist must discover that the

public has a secret mind of its own. Nothing can

tell him the way to find that public mind better than

his own courage and his own ingenuity. The word NEW

in newspapers must remain the predominant theme.

———————

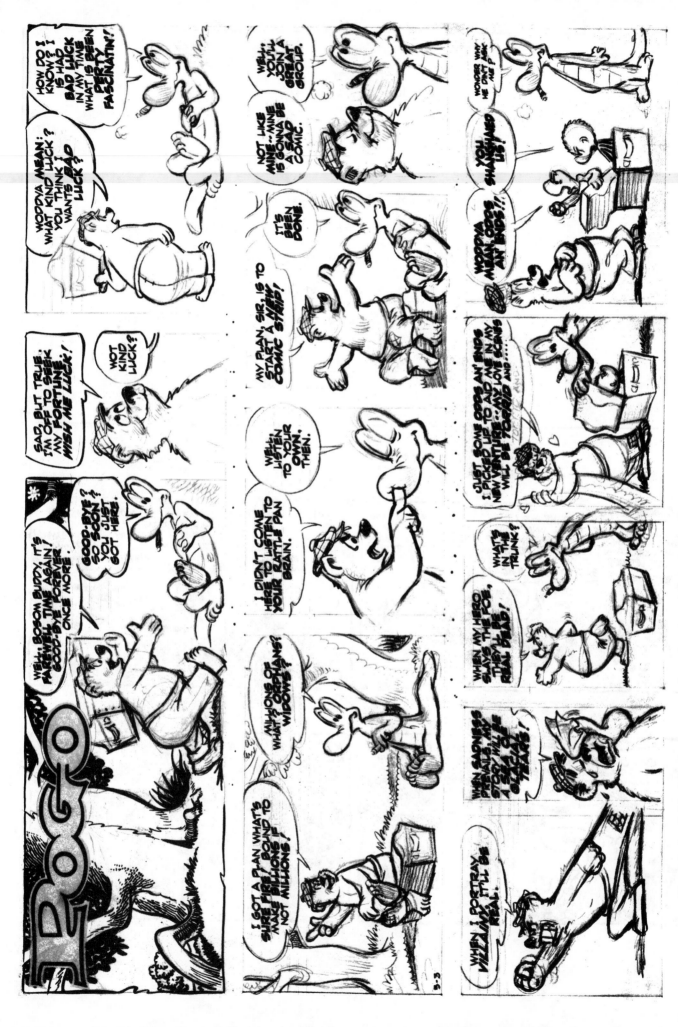

When viewing finished Sunday pages, readers often forget about the penciling underneath the ink. Selby Kelly unearthed this stat of a Sunday strip that has been penciled and lettered but awaits final inking.

8-6 PUBLISHERS-HALL SYNDICATE

HOW COME THE BIG FAT "ROWR"?

YOU, MY OL' PAL AN' BOSOM COMPANION! I CAN'T GET NO CO-OPERATION FROM EVEN UNTO YOU, MY OL' PAL AND ETC.

ROWR!

ALL'S I WANT TO DO IS HAVE YOU, MY BOSOM ETCETERA PAL, JUST PLAY BALL ON WHAT MY BIG PROJECT IS ABOUT··· TO COMMUNICATE CULTURE EE-LECTRONIWOCKLE-WISE TO THE MASSES!

I'LL DO IT, DO IT, DO IT, DO IT!

OKAY, NOW YOU GETS OFF AN' TELEFORMS ME TO ASK CULTURAL QUESTIONS DURIN' MY CULTURAL RADIO PROGRAM···

RIGHTIO

10-3   THE HALL SYNDICATE

WELL, FRIENDS, HERE WE IS, ON OUR BIG FAT QUESTION PROGRAM··· BUT FIRST, A SONG···

♪ LISTEN, YOU LOVERS 2 AN' DANCERS AN' PRANCERS, 'PHONE UNCLE OWL TO GET ALL THE ANSWERS··· ♪ I'M SMART AN' I'M BRIGHT AN' MY ANSWERS ARE RIGHT AN' I··· HOLD THE FOAM!

HELLO!?

DEAR SIR: HOW WOULD YOU HANDLE A BIG-MOUTH, KNOW-IT-ALL CHILD WHAT'S TOO BIG FOR HIS BRIDGES? YOURS TRULY, A FRIEND.

YES, A FRIEND! NORMALLY, ONE WOULD WISH TO AVOID BRUISIN' THE TRAUMA OF THE LI'L SPRAT, BUT DOCTOR OWL HERE FEELS WE INDULGES THESE SCAPERS TOO MUCH···

TAKE THIS BUM AN' THRASTLE HIM··· PLADGE HIS BANDLES! SPLARSH A BUCKET OF WATER ON HIS NUMP AN'···

THIS WILL NOT ONLY STOP HIM, IT WILL GIVE YOU VAST SATISFACTION AN'···

SPLARSH!

MAN! HE'S RIGHT ON THAT "VAST SATISFACTION" JAZZ.

HELLO?

POEMS OF THE POSSUM

THE HAZY YON

How pierceful grows the hazy yon!
How myrtle petaled thou!
For spring hath sprung the Cyclotron,
How high browse thou, brown cow?

1950

MANY HAPPY RETURNS

Once you were two,
Dear birthday friend,
In spite of purple weather.

But now you are three
And near the end
As we grewsome together.

How fourthful thou,
Forsooth for you,
For soon you will be more!

But—'fore
One can be three be two;
Before be five be four!

1951

THE OLYMPICS

We salute you, oh, games of the ages
But the game of an age turning gray
Was when I carried the torch on Veronica's porch
In the city of Athens, Ga.

1957

LINES UPON A TRANQUIL BROW

Have you ever, while pondering the ways of the morn,
Thought to save just a bit, just a drop in the horn,
To pour in the evening or late afternoon
Or during the night when we're shining the moon?
Have you ever cried out, while counting the snow,
Or watching the tomtit warble hello . . .
"Break out the cigars, this life is for squirrels;
We're off to the drugstore to whistle at girls"
                    ?
                                        1955

THE MARKED AND
BURNING DECK

Gamboling on the gumbo
With the gambits all in gear,
I daffed upon a dilly
Who would be my dolly dear.

Oh, Dilly, I would dally
If you'd be but truly true.
How silly, I must sally
Off to do my duly do.

1954

NORTHERN LIGHTS

Oh, roar a roar for Nora,
Nora Alice in the night.
For she has seen Aurora
Borealis burning bright.

A furore for our Nora!
And applaud Aurora seen!
Where, throughout the Summer, has
Our Borealis been?

1953

ALI BABA THE BLACK SHEEP

The Keen and the Quing were quirling at quoits
In the meadow behind of the mere.
Tho' mainly the meadow was middled with mow,
An heretical hitherto here.

The Prince and the Princess were plaiting the plates
And prating quite primly the peer.
And that's why the Duchess stuck ducks on the Duke
For no one was over to seer.

1954

TWIRL, TWIRL

Twirl! Twirl! Twinkle between!
The tweezers are twist in the twittering twain.
Twirl! Twirl! Entwiningly twirl
'Twixt twice twenty twigs passing platitudes plain.
Plunder the plover and rover rides round.
Ring all the rungs on the brassily bound,
Billy, Swirl! Swirl! Swingingly swirl!
Sweep along swoop along sweetly your swain.

1956

MAN'S BEST FRIEND

What gentler eye, what nobler heart
Doth warm the winter day
Than the true blue orb and the oaken core
Of beloved old dog Tray?

1951

Ideas, Inc.

by Walt Kelly

WHERE do you get your ideas?" they ask. I don't know whether novelists, playwrights, bank robbers or poets are asked the same question, but it certainly is the common question asked of every cartoonist.

If the question were asked in a fitting sense of awe, I would be a happier man. However, it seems to be prompted by the opinion that the cartoonist just doesn't look bright enough to have any ideas at all. The questioner is often a man who attempts to conceal his boredom as he surveys the comic-strip artist. Can this, he seems to ask himself, be a person who pays more income tax than I do? Me, with my college education, my own dry-cleaning shop and my collection of Ethel M. Dell first editions?

Intellectual-type females will often ask the question, too. They sort of dare you to answer, knowing your reply will be a ham-handed lie. Fortunately they have no real interest in you except as an example of what unplanned breeding can do to the human race. After a steady myopic stare at you through a set of sequined spectacles, they retire to the company of other never-married divorcees to discuss something in bad French.

Usually a cartoonist gets his ideas out of the trash bin of his own brain. For example, the verses that follow all came from the odd look of a word placed against a word not usually seen in its company: "Mustache of the Grass," "Pumpkin Tree," etc. Then some words look juicy by themselves: "boodle," "boon," "loot."

You search for incongruity in your head, but sometimes it comes readily to hand. You'll recall that this past year, Garth Williams, the illustrator and writer of children's books, in his naïveté thought there was nothing wrong with a black bunny marrying a white rabbit. After his viewpoint was contested and the book put under lock and key in a Southern public library, the case of the three little pigs came up.

Whitman Publishing, of Racine, Wis., had published a version of this old favorite story employing a white pig, a spotted or "mulatto" pig, and a black pig. The constituent of a Florida legislator had complained that up until six or seven years ago these pigs were all white. In a letter of protest to my friend Lloyd Smith, the publisher, the congressman had wanted to know what had caused the change. There seemed to be some devious parallel being drawn (one Southerner called it "brainwashing"). All these people were aroused because it was the black pig in several versions who usually outwitted the wolf. If it wasn't he, it was the mulatto pig. The white pig was clearly being discriminated against. Mr. Smith replied that so far he'd not been able to see much resemblance between pigs and human beings.

The congressman was not amused. He wrote a stern letter in which he demanded that the name of the author be divulged so that the congressman, on behalf of himself and his constituent, might learn whether the story had been written under orders from higher up. Otherwise, he suggested, the whole matter might be referred to committee for interrogation.

Much of this, except the suggestion that a Congressional committee might be interested, found its way into the papers.

The Whitman book was held up for examination, and gleeful reporters kept Mr. Smith busy answering questions for a few days. Some of the newspapers agreed that the whole question made a pretty mixed-up kid out of the zebra and that all zoos should be careful. Weary at last, Lloyd said to the last reporter who called long distance, "Do you drink Scotch or Bourbon?" The reporter eagerly and hopefully answered that he drank Scotch. "Well, we're all going to look pretty silly from now on ordering White and White," said Smith gloomily.

You want to know where we get our ridiculous ideas? That's where, right out of one horn of plenty or another.

— 220 —

POGO LIVES ON
WITH
FIRESIDE
BOOKS

___ OUTRAGEOUSLY POGO
by Mrs. Walt Kelly and Bill Crouch, Jr.
0-671-55374-7 $9.95

___ THE BEST OF POGO
by Mrs. Walt Kelly and Bill Crouch, Jr.
0-671-42796-2 $9.95

___ POGO EVEN BETTER
by Mrs. Walt Kelly and Bill Crouch, Jr.
0-671-50473-8 $9.95

___ TEN EVER-LOVIN' BLUE-EYED YEARS WITH POGO
by Walt Kelly
0-671-21428-4 $11.95

___ POGO: WE HAVE MET THE ENEMY AND HE IS US
by Walt Kelly
0-671-21260-5 $6.95

___ POGO ROMANCES RECAPTURED
by Walt Kelly
0-671-22184-1 $9.95

___ POGO'S DOUBLE SUNDAE
by Walt Kelly
0-671-24139-7 $9.95

___ POGO WILL BE THAT WAS
by Walt Kelly
0-671-24854-5 $9.95

___ PLUPERFECT POGO
by Walt Kelly
0-671-64220-0-0 $10.95

Simon & Schuster, Inc.
200 Old Tappan Road
Old Tappan, NJ 07675. Mail Order Dept. P6
Please send me copies of the above titles. (Indicate quantities in boxes above. If not completely satisfied, you may return for full refund within 14 days.)
☐ Save! Enclose full amount per copy with this coupon. Publisher pays postage and handling; or charge my credit card.
☐ Master Card ☐ Visa

My credit card number is _____ Card expires _____
Signature _____
Name _____
(Please Print)
Address _____
City _____ State _____ Zip Code _____
or available at your local bookstore

Prices subject to change without notice.